Pathways to
STILLNESS

REFLECT, RELEASE, RENEW

Gary Irwin-Kenyon, PhD

◆ FriesenPress

Suite 300 - 990 Fort St
Victoria, BC, V8V 3K2
Canada

www.friesenpress.com

ISBN
978-1-4602-8899-3 (Hardcover)
978-1-4602-8900-6 (Paperback)
978-1-4602-8901-3 (eBook)

1. SELF-HELP

Distributed to the trade by The Ingram Book Company

DEDICATION

To my teachers for the gift of their generosity and
patience, and to Jimmy, Raymond, and Clifford.

In stillness, the world is restored.

—Lao Tzu, *The Tao Te Ching*

TABLE OF CONTENTS

ACKNOWLEDGEMENTS

THE journey of writing this book has been a solitary, and at times, lonely affair—as is generally said about the writing life. I found that I needed to find some stillness in order to write about it. However, I have been accompanied by many on this journey.

First and foremost, I thank my wife, Liz, for her encouragement, emotional support, and practical wisdom; I also must thank my daughters, Christina and Jessica.

Early on in my musings about stillness, my good friend and colleague Bill Randall told me that I *must* write this book. He has shared my enthusiasm and has been a sounding board at important times throughout the process. I treasure our friendship and professional collaboration, which I have enjoyed for over twenty years. I am also very thankful to my first readers, who agreed to provide me with a candid assessment of the manuscript. I am particularly grateful to my friends Ardeth Holmes, Geoff Slater, and Rodrigo Gutierrez-Hermelo, who provided me with detailed and insightful suggestions, and who also shared my enthusiasm for the project. I also thank Jim Kesel, Sylvie Guenette and Marc Swan. In addition, many thanks go to Doug Vipond for his excellent copyediting,

Matthew Steeves for the cover photo, and to Glen Ross for the Tai Chi photos. Finally, I would like to express my appreciation to the editorial staff at Friesen Press who have been accessible, friendly, and who "get" the book.

INTRODUCTION

THIS book is the result of many other intersecting journeys. First, there is the journey of my own life, which led to the desire to write about stillness. Then, there are the lives that have touched me in special ways: gerontology students in my university classes, older adults in the community, my Tai Chi friends in long-term care. Still another interesting part of the journey of this book is that as soon as I began to talk to acquaintances and friends about how I was writing this book, they would start to share an experience of stillness, describe what the word meant to them, or say that it reminded them to pay more attention to their own pathways to stillness.

This book is about stillness—what it is, how you can find it, where it hides itself, why it is necessary to your life. It is a beginner's guide because, with stillness, no experience is necessary. Besides, you are always a beginner; when stillness is present, there truly is nothing to do and nowhere to go.

This book is also about learning to appreciate wandering or meandering along life's pathways. It does not contain Six Easy Steps to Wisdom and Immortality. Rather, it offers a way to approach your journey, which you then create and discover on your own, with help. On this journey, you often cannot see what is around the next bend. But if you show up, it can be a journey of curiosity, wonder, and more life. You may come to agree with Tolkien's words, "All who wander are not lost."

Reflecting on much of my personal and professional life, I have—first unconsciously, then increasingly consciously—realized that I started looking for someone or something to save me, to make everything all right: a place, a philosophical viewpoint, a girlfriend, a job, money, a particular skill, a particular teacher or guru, and even my own thoughts. I have now arrived at the point in my journey where I observe that none of these options are very good candidates for bringing lasting meaning and peace to my life. Since they are dependent on outside factors and conditions, they represent, more accurately, a project likely doomed to failure, frustration, and disillusionment. I have begun to realize—little by little, and by way of many rounds of things not quite going my way—that I do *not* need saving, that everything is all right as long as I can live without a final answer. All the outside circumstances or forms are great to learn from, can be very enjoyable, and are an integral part of the journey. However, they are fickle as permanent companions. That is, except for the answer of stillness.

Stillness does not let you down, because it is not dependent on anything else, even though it often shows itself in people, places, and things. In this way, stillness is not the same thing as happiness. Happiness is about the satisfaction of expectations and desires. "If only I could get that job," or "When my mortgage is paid off," or "If only I could find love," or "If only the neighbour from hell would move away"—then I will be happy. But true happiness is not what you think. Stillness brings a measure of lasting joy, but happiness often brings only temporary peace, since it is attached to outside conditions and your own expectations. You can experience deep stillness and peace even when the world is not behaving according to your plan. Perhaps this is the "peace that surpasses understanding" that Jesus talked about.

The experience and practice of stillness has helped me see the outer aspects of my life in a gentler and kinder way; thus I have become less discontent and fearful, and I experience more joy and contentment in my life. This may not seem like much, but it is mine. However, this does not mean I am fearless, doubtless, anxiety free, or without confusion; on the contrary, I am also challenged, clumsy, and frail in particular areas of my life. But when stillness is part of the picture, the relentless change that makes up my life is embraced in a different way.

I think about those from whom I have learned much: the Dalai Lama, Eckhart Tolle, St. Therese of Lisieux, Thich Nhat Hanh, Thomas Merton, and other Buddhist and Taoist writers, some who wrote centuries ago. Then there are the students who have written reflection papers in my university courses for the past thirty years. They have expressed their wisdom in words that have inspired, consoled, and made me feel that they are kindred spirits on this journey to life. And so while I had some initial hesitation in publishing this book, I now feel free to add my voice to this chorus of expression with something that reflects my own combination of insights and life story. I also wanted to share this with a wider audience because, in my observation, there are not so many books on stillness.

So why should there be yet another book on the spiritual life? The simple answer is that navigating this journey of life is incredibly challenging, and I feel a strong desire to share whatever modest insights I have gained along the way in the hope that they are of benefit to others. You and I are faced with overwhelming global issues, including the unstable world economy, climate change, and various actual and possible military conflicts. We all need a practical and personal way to be quiet, to rest, and to observe. That way comes from reminding ourselves regularly that we have access to stillness. We need to learn how to *be* with change, and to quietly sit with the painful and unpleasant.

I have come to experience and respect stillness in three ways: through personal experience, through a particular spiritual tradition, and through my profession as a gerontology professor. Over the years, each way has helped to deepen my understanding of the others.

One of my "signature stories" (as my colleague, Bill Randall, and I call them) is based on personal experience: my divorce, which happened over twenty years ago. Before this event, I felt that I'd always had control over everything in my life, so I presumed that, one way or another, I could deal with whatever came up. But as it turned out, I was overcome with anxiety, fear, loneliness, and confusion during this time. The rug was pulled out from under me, and I was lost and in great pain.

This experience was particularly distressing to me as I assumed that, with my martial arts background, I would prevail. But I had some new lessons to learn. These new insights began with a telephone call from my *sensei* (teacher) Earl, who had moved to another city, and who had heard about my situation. I will never forget this call. He said that what I had to do was simply survive from minute to minute, hour to hour, day to day. I had to give in to what was happening, not resist, fight, or try to control. This part of my journey, which lasted for approximately one year (and led me to a new, loving partner and two children) sparked my interest in what this book is about.

The second lesson on stillness came through my practice of martial arts, especially Tai Chi. I have been curious about the meaning of life and death for most of my adult life and have learned much from my studies of a variety of wisdom traditions. Tai Chi is a particularly effective pathway to stillness for me, with its emphasis on yielding, following, and letting go. In partner training in Tai Chi, if you apply brute strength or muscle power with a partner who has learned to yield, you will, in most cases, lose. Contrary to what we tend to think, particularly in Western culture, to yield and let go is not equivalent to weakness or failure.

My third lesson on stillness comes from adult students of all ages in the courses I teach at university. In particular, I teach a course called *Death and Dying*, and another called *Aging and Tai Chi*. In these courses students write an autobiographical paper on their experiences and opinions about meaning in life, spiritual experiences, loss, grief, and end-of-life issues. It may sound strange, but the *Death and Dying* course is one of my favourite courses to teach. The reason is that each year I am honoured and deeply moved by the stories that students share with me. The themes of these stories range from the death of a loved grandparent, to the suicide of a close friend, to dealing with a serious illness or injury of their own, to a broken or abusive relationship. In most of these stories there is a described movement from—though they do not use these terms necessarily—pain and suffering, to acceptance and surrender, to new meaning, sensitivity to other persons, compassion, and an appreciation of stillness.

These students often express gratitude at having a chance to tell their story, as they seldom have the opportunity to do so at home or with friends. This speaks to the need for an enhanced cultural dialogue on these aspects of the human condition. It is my hope that this book will provide an answer to those who question why anyone would want to study what they consider such a morbid topic.

Finally, I have learned a great deal about this less-explored territory of human life through my many relationships with older persons in the community—some friends, some colleagues, and some strangers—during the past thirty years working both as a gerontologist and as a Tai Chi teacher. In listening to the stories of their journeys, I have learned that what may look like one thing on the outside may be very different from the inside, even in extreme circumstances such as dementia. I believe that we need to look at the process of aging more from the inside than we have thus far. When aging is viewed as a lifelong process of change, the journey of aging *is* the journey to life. It can be a very effective gateway, or, as

Eckhart Tolle would say, a portal to stillness. The anti-aging movement as a mechanism of control only postpones the inevitable from the outside, and perhaps also postpones the possibility of finding other forms of richness in the human journey. This book is for those who are curious about this journey to life.

Before going any further, I would like to acknowledge the possibility that it may be quite foolish for me to think that I have something valuable to say about such concepts as stillness and wisdom. As I explore this topic, I feel the philosopher Ludwig Wittgenstein's admonition in my consciousness, warning me that perhaps we should remain silent about that of which we cannot speak; I also bear in mind the Taoist admonition that the Tao of which we speak is not itself the Tao. Nevertheless, having made this qualification, I feel free to continue, since I believe that, for human beings, stillness is only accessible through our senses and language, provided you take them as signposts and not ultimate reality or truth. Stillness is not a disembodied serenity, but a way of living in a complex and complicated world.

The characters in this story are wide-ranging in their origins. You will hear voices from Christianity, Tai Chi, and secular spiritual thinkers, as well as our fellow travellers on the journey. In this respect, there is a second purpose to the book: I would like it to contribute to the ecumenical movement, which is necessary today. I hope to contribute to the insight that God has no particular costume, or, conversely, that God is present in all traditions; ultimately, God is present in each of our unique wisdom stories. You may or may not choose to belong to a particular organized religion.

Your personal journey may consist of a meaningful way of life that combines a number of traditions or perspectives.

This book brings traditional ideas into the twenty-first century, both in the insights themselves and in the format of the book. The themes explored here—spirituality, journey, story, and stillness—are timeless and time-honoured, but never more needed than now in this postmodern world, with its overload of information along with an epidemic of a sense of meaninglessness.

Why stillness?

When a problem arises in our lives, we most often use our thinking minds to seek out an answer, a solution external to ourselves, whether it be a medication, an expert with a PhD, or a technique downloaded from the Internet. We need to find a way to maintain control over any situation. If we find that we cannot solve a problem in these ways, we begin to feel that there is no way out, that we are stuck and in pain. Very often, we also feel that we have failed, not measured up to the challenge. Self-blame creeps into the picture.

The next step in this process is to deny that the problem is there. Or we continue to look only outside for answers and expect a quick fix to quell the pain. I call this *comfort behaviour*. There are many forms of comfort behaviour; they mostly represent the plethora of ills that characterize postmodern society. The list includes substance abuse in its many forms—from food to drugs and alcohol to smoking; television and Internet overuse; gambling; pornography; spousal abuse. Another common comfort behaviour is to simply fill every moment with some kind of activity, just to stay busy.

The truth of this statement was brought home to me by the following story: Years ago, when I was between degrees and working for a bank as a management trainee, we were all called to a meeting for an announcement. The head manager said that there was going to be a specialist visiting the branch to do a stress workshop for us. One of my colleagues spoke up immediately, red-faced and very upset. He said, "I do not have any [expletive] time for a [expletive] stress workshop!" You may agree that this is a very common experience in today's workplace.

If these are not the comfort behaviours of choice, then we may just feel depressed and live a life of quiet desperation. Whatever the comfort behaviours, they mask fear, a sense of meaninglessness, and a lack of peace in our lives. We are very often on the run, seeking some way to escape the present moment that is felt to be unsatisfactory, if we are aware of it at all. The author John O'Donohue puts it well when he says that when we accumulate experiences so fast, everything becomes thin. Consequently, we are not in touch with our own lives, and this creates a sense of meaninglessness and emptiness. We do not consider stillness as a solution to our problems because it requires that we simply stop *doing*, let go, and *be*—a strategy that, if considered at all, seems completely contradictory and unproductive. Nevertheless, at the same time, your life is all stress and no stillness.

Of course, there are solutions to many human problems that we can and should seek outside ourselves. I would also like to say at the outset that we all do what we need to do to get through the day. My main argument is that we often do not include enough stillness or compassion in our self- and other- evaluations. We can be too hard on ourselves.

Some forms and degrees of comfort behaviour are welcome, even healthy. The trick is to discover a comfort behaviour that is actually good for us. We do need to have fun! In the bank example earlier, the routine on a Friday afternoon was for the managers to gather in an office and take out a bottle of Scotch and put it on the desk. A drink after a hard week of work may be appropriate; however, they would drink for a couple of hours and then go to the local pub and not go home until very late. In this case, a measure of release and comfort may turn into a source of suffering for you and for those around you. This book will be of interest to those who would like to suffer less.

There are many human dilemmas and questions that are more appropriately termed mysteries than problems. As examples, there are the mysteries surrounding the meaning of human aging, dying, and death. What do you do if you receive a diagnosis of Alzheimer's disease or a terminal illness? How does a mother deal with the discovery that her daughter is a drug addict? How do you manage loneliness? More generally, does the journey of life and aging provide you with an opportunity for spiritual growth, or only dissolution and despair? It is said that the journey of the spirit involves loss toward meaning; does the journey of life do the same? Is it possible to embrace human aging as a spiritual journey to *more* life, not less?

In a culture that glorifies control, a book about stillness sounds like a book about nothing. Perhaps it is, in a Seinfeld way! Stillness is no-thing, as you will see. Priest, professor of theology, and author

Martin Laird elegantly describes stillness as "a sunlit absence." In any case, there is benefit to looking in detail at simple things that are very close to you in a different way. When dealing with the mysteries of life, we are compelled to look inside as well as outside. Now, looking inside involves a process that can be variously called surrendering, letting go, giving in, accepting, yielding, allowing. This may sound like a way to give up and fall into depression, since there is no way to fix or control important parts of our lives. But happiness, meaning, spirituality, wisdom and peace have more to do with first losing in order to gain, more with emptying than accumulating, more with space than form. Through this process you can discover that what is left is not nothing. Still, this could indeed be seen as a book about nothing: nothing to control, nowhere to go; as a yoga teacher once said, "There is nothing next."

Because stillness is no-thing—the opposite of doing—it can be quite disconcerting when you first experience it. You may find that you want to go back to the busyness, the old fears, or the crisis mode with which you are more familiar. Yet stillness has its own momentum; its logic builds within you the more you show up for it. Eventually, you may learn to trust the peace inside, and find it even in the midst of the noise of life. You may find that once you taste stillness, you notice it when it goes missing. You may find yourself choosing people, places, and situations of stillness. You may find that you do not enjoy being pulled away from the experience of stillness. But life happens, so it is a matter of finding it where you can, in your inside story, or in the larger story you live within.

I decided to write this book because I realized that I need to be constantly reminded about this important part of my journey. Everyday life provides us with endless forms of distraction and opportunities to forget, or to remain unconscious to our own stillness. Different words reach different people at different times; no one else knows what it takes for another person to open the door to their own journey. You often do not know what kind of an impact you are having on one another, for better or worse. Being a teacher, I have often felt that I was giving and not receiving much in return in terms of feedback. However, often—even years after the fact—a student will contact me and express how much they appreciated our time together. When it comes to these topics, we need only trust that we have something to say that might be of use to at least one other traveller.

In addition, the world desperately needs insights that bring together divergent traditions toward what Aldous Huxley calls the perennial philosophy. We need to learn to use our words as signs that point to common experiences of communion, wisdom, and love. This direction is vital, because you find meaning only through your own inside story, as part of a journey that is paradoxically both unique and shared with all members of the species. From this point of view, specific religious and spiritual paths are stories that each of us finds more or less inspiring, based on our personalities, interests, and cultural experiences.

The stories are signposts that point to a personal and universal experience of stillness. You may find comfort and meaning in Jesus, in the Buddha, or in a more nature-based story such as Taoism. Or you may find it in Oprah or Dr. Phil. A great deal of suffering in the world today is the result of people mistaking the signpost for the reality. It is as though there are many alternative itineraries to reach a particular destination, and each path is blind to any but its own.

In this book, I invite you to simply show up and let stillness happen. Stillness finds you more than you find it. It has its own rules. Nevertheless, you can create conditions that will make it more likely that you will experience stillness. Like electricity, you do not need to understand stillness to experience its benefits. It is mostly about showing up. Each chapter of this book contains two ways to invite stillness into your life.

Throughout the book, you will read about how stillness works and how people have found stillness. These reflections also highlight misconceptions about the journey to life, which includes the changes that occur the longer your journey is in clock time. These misconceptions can often hold you back from encountering stillness. Perhaps you have not found stillness because you have not been looking in the right place. Again, happiness is not what we often think it is. It may be possible to find stillness and peace and not necessarily be *happy*. By understanding your life as a story, you can become more patient, compassionate, and accepting of your own journey. You can even observe your life with humour at times, especially as you realize that (speaking for myself, at least) you do not really know very much. Unknowing can be a strength rather than a weakness.

Stillness is an experience, not an idea. Sometimes you need to do something, or sometimes you need to do nothing. The way to stillness is through calming down, quieting what has been called the "monkey mind." Thus at the end of the book there are three easy-to-learn Tai Chi movements for relaxing into stillness. The movements may be performed from either a standing or seated position. They can in themselves bring about stillness in your life.

It is my hope that by reading this book you will learn how to see your life as a story. This does not mean that the story of your life is *only* a story in a trivial sense. Rather, it means that you think, feel, and act on the basis of a story that you tell yourself, and others, about something or someone. If so, then it is possible for your stories to be changed. Unlike clock time, story time allows you to find new meaning in the present and to change your past toward a different future. You will see how this can work for you as this story unfolds. In addition, many chapters take things one step further and give you specific guidelines to explore your pathway.

While we each have our own unique journey to life, we share many common station stops as we change over the lifespan—that is, on our common existential ride. These station stops occur in two different parts of your life: your inner self, or your inside story, and the larger story that you live within. This includes your relationships with others, as well as the world as a whole. In these two areas there are both challenges and potentials as your journey continues.

The purpose of this book is to show you how the meaning of these stories may change for the better for you when seen from the point of view of stillness and your own ordinary wisdom. Ordinary wisdom is the wisdom you create and discover within your unique path. Aging is also about change, and many of these changes can bring you to stillness and moments of peace if you look at them from the points of view of meaning, attitude, and technology. This is what I call the MAT concept. The idea is that if you can find a better story to live by—and therefore age meaningfully by—you will find more stillness.

To pull these threads together, as you read each stillness story you are invited to try a "relax into stillness" movement.

You relax into stillness for its own sake, but also in order to create a space in which to comfortably read your life story, as well as learn from the stories of fellow travellers. Unless you are totally happy with things as they are, you can stop simply living the story you *have been* until now and open your sense of what is possible, and discover new meaning. These insights then bring you full circle to more stillness in your life.

It helps to remind ourselves as we go through this book that we are only human, that there is no perfection, and that expectations need to be tempered with compassion, humour, and forgiveness. We are often flawed and frail, yet hard to knock out. Again, stillness works by its own rules, but there are often wonderful surprises when you least expect it. All you can do is show up and be open.

This book is not a traditional story with a beginning, middle, and end. Feel free to read the book in any order that suits you, and return to those chapters, and relax-into-stillness movements that speak to you more than others. Enjoy discovering a pathway to stillness that fits *your* life. This is a book that can be read while waiting for an appointment, or before going to sleep, or when you have a few minutes to yourself, or when you can steal a few minutes.

PART A:
Meaningful Aging

The stillness stories in this section are about pathways of meaningful aging, the journey to life, and the story of your life.

CHAPTER 1
Divorce and New Life

AFTER going through a nasty divorce, I was thrown into complete confusion and anxiety for about a year. As my sister once said, I lost my story. I could not decide anything, including whether to keep on working at my university teaching job. I could not sleep, and I could not concentrate. At the beginning I could not even lift weights, which I tried to do in the gym in my new apartment building, after I lost the house. It was at this time that I received the phone call from my sensei, Earl, whom I mentioned earlier; he told me to just survive from minute to minute, and hour to hour.

What sort of crazy advice was my macho karate teacher giving me—to accept, to give in, to not resist what was happening? I was accustomed to working my way out of problems with more kicks and punches or running or otherwise figuring it out. I was used to being in control. But this was an experience I could not control. Still, I somehow listened to Earl's advice. I was dimly aware that I could not fix this problem quickly and perhaps needed another approach. It did not make me feel any better physically, but the support from a good friend was welcome. I did not feel so alone. And so I began to pay attention to the concept of stillness.

A bit later in this journey, a colleague (who was also a priest) told me about a Trappist monastery in northern New Brunswick, where there was a monk who might be good for me to meet. So I went there for a couple of weeks. I worked in the barn, cleaning out cow stalls and performing other jobs, which did feel good. The special experience, though, was meeting Brother Henry. I asked if I could speak with him, and we went for several walks on the monastery grounds. I explained my situation. He did not say much, though he did talk a bit about his own life and how he arrived at the monastery. I was struck by how I felt an absence of anxiety and confusion while in his presence. I could not understand this, but I was able to find some stillness during these walks. (Eventually I began writing this book at the monastery, which has become one of my refuges or "stillness environments." The atmosphere there gives me a feeling of safety, comfort, acceptance, and peace. It is a place of silence and love, both in the building and on the grounds. It is a place to rest and to allow life to happen.)

These experiences—and the company of a few good, accepting friends—helped me to get out of my crazy and fearful monkey mind. But I was still in bad shape emotionally and needed another kind of help. A good friend and colleague, Warren, who is a physician, talked to me and subsequently drove up to the monastery a couple of hours from his home with some medication to calm my nerves and help me sleep. I hated to take any pills, so I resisted this advice. But then he reminded me that he was not a pill doctor, and that he believed in the wise use of medication. I accepted this advice, and it gave me much relief.

These are only some of the experiences and people I encountered during this time, which was over twenty years ago. However, since this experience I have become increasingly aware of, and interested in, the place of stillness in my own life and in my personal and professional encounters with others. Gradually, I have learned that acceptance, surrender, giving in, or yielding—which appear like weakness and resignation—actually result in much wisdom and strength *through* loss. Moreover, I have learned that we can get better at this *third way*, beyond fight and flight. Happiness is not what you think. It is not about the total satisfaction of desires or expectations; it is about being okay even when you are not okay. It is about discovering stillness in the chaos.

Explore your Pathway

Is there an experience in your life where you could consider adopting the third way: accepting, giving-in, being open to help from the larger story you live within? The relax-into-stillness movements at the end of the book could assist you in this process.

CHAPTER 2
Meaningful Suffering?

WHAT about suffering? It is not necessary to suffer to find stillness, yet it is a very common pathway. At first glance, you may consider all suffering to be unwelcome. You may feel it to be unnecessary, that you do not deserve it, and that you need to resist or deny it. You may attempt to avoid suffering in yourself and feel uncomfortable around others who appear to be suffering.

This avoidance can be taken to the extreme of what thanatologists (those who study end-of-life issues) call *social death*. This means that you treat a person as an object, as if they were already gone. Social death is experienced by many, including terminally ill persons, dementia survivors, visible minorities, older persons, and disabled persons. Research tells us that many of our fellow travellers in these circumstances say that the most difficult challenge they face originates in the way others treat them. The frailty or disability is not the biggest problem—other people are! When you suffer, the initial movement is one of closing off, feeling separate and alienated, disconnected from yourself, your family, your community, and even God. This situation is captured in the title of a journal article by the pioneering narrative medicine physician Harold Brody: "My Story Is Broken: Can You Help Me Fix It?"

Suffering changes your story—your *whole* story—not just the part affected by the loss. And what can be even more disturbing are the times that you experience multiple suffering—more than one thing happening at once. This is sometimes called *bereavement overload*. As one ninety-three-year-old gentleman said to me, "I should have been dead a long time ago, but God has not finished beating me up." He was referring to the loss of his partner, his health issues, and his financial troubles. Suffering is a part of your journey. But it tends to make us feel stuck or trapped with no way out, in a *prison-like situation*, as, for example, Helen Black's participants characterize it in her study of suffering in later life.

You are stuck until you are willing to entertain the possibility that you are more than your ego and its need for control, which gets expressed through your thinking mind, your monkey mind. Curiously enough, it is suffering that most often brings you to the point of considering this possibility. It is at this point in the journey that you may discover a purpose to suffering. One way to put this is that your old story dies so a new one can be born, one that brings you less suffering and more stillness. And though our natural instinct is to resist giving up the old story—after all, we are attached to it and really do not want a new story!—the potential of a new story deserves a closer look. In my experience, in spite of (or, more correctly, because of) suffering, loss, confusion, mistakes, and wrong roads taken, life clarifies itself on the journey.

It is worth noting that there are stories of spiritual practitioners throughout history who have sought out pain and deprivation, because they believed it brought them closer to God. As David Bromberg sings, "You've got to suffer if you wanna sing the blues." (In fact, I have known a couple of artists who seem to regularly invite chaos into their lives with the idea that it will make their art better.) But I agree with Eckhart Tolle, who says that deliberately sought suffering often strengthens the ego through a sense of achievement (i.e., *Look at me—I can take it!*). This is counterproductive to a pathway to stillness. It is suffering that happens *to* you, and that is unwelcome, that has more potential to help you to find meaning and stillness. Perhaps this is because you cannot take credit for it. Nevertheless, you may say, along with my monk friend, Brother Leo, that you would rather get it over with now, so that there will be more stillness later.

But, in most cases, we don't usually or consciously seek out pain and suffering. As Jean Vanier, the spiritual teacher and founder of L'Arche, a network of homes for adults with special abilities, tells us, our spontaneous reaction to suffering is most often repulsion. We are naturally frightened of pain, so the most common response is to deny it and avoid it at all costs. This is particularly the case when the suffering or *cross* is beyond our capabilities. When you suffer but can still handle things, you might feel that this is good for your self-development or character. But, as I have found, it may be a different story when it is suffering that pulls the rug out from under you. You may just want it to go away or for you to get away, anyhow or any way.

The way forward with this journey is to find a middle ground—a third way between a desire for suffering and a complete denial or desire to escape from pain. This third way operates by relaxing into stillness and appreciating stillness stories—most importantly, *your own.*

There are good reasons for you to believe that suffering is absurd and that it should be avoided at all costs. But if you are willing to take a second look at it, you may be surprised at what you find. As our culture becomes less fearful of *being with* suffering, and as more of us tell our stories, the list of examples grows longer. There are more and more stories emerging on the scene by those of you who have suffered and are willing to share your ordinary wisdom—share the way that suffering has brought you to meaning and stillness. Besides the other stories you find in this book, here are some examples that I have discovered.

I was recently asked to contribute a commentary to an academic journal on research that was carried out based on an analysis of life stories of Holocaust survivors. One of the findings of this research is that, for many survivors, the stereotype of said survivors being in the throes of depression, having post-traumatic stress disorder (PTSD), and suffering from a sense of meaninglessness turns out to be just that—a stereotype. Many of the survivors have actually gone on to healthy, meaningful lives and lives of service to others. This research lends further support to the views of Viktor Frankl, himself a survivor, whose life and work demonstrated the ability of the human spirit to discover meaning in seemingly hopeless circumstances. For Frankl, meaninglessness itself is a source of pain, spiritual malaise, depression, and despair. In fact, Frankl speaks about an equation he created: $D = S - M$ (Despair equals Suffering minus Meaning). I would also recommend the film *The Lady in Number Six*, in which Alice, a 109-year-old survivor, tells her story of how music brought her stillness in utter chaos.

Besides the Holocaust, the *suffering* list includes studies of widowhood, dementia, depression, disability, frailty, and substance and other forms of abuse. In my own work with guided autobiography, a program created by the pioneering gerontologist Jim Birren, I have been honoured to have people share personal stories of loss, pain, grief, and new meaning. In a course in which I participated in Los Angeles, an older Hispanic man shared his story of having lost his son years earlier, when the son, a concert pianist, was twenty-five years of age. This gentleman told of being devastated, as anyone would be, and he added that in his culture, it is particularly traumatic to lose a son. He was now able to tell this story and he said it gave him some peace to do so, as it might help others.

We also heard from another participant, who told of her experiences of sexual abuse as a child. While telling the story, she began to cry, and I was worried that she might be at risk because this was a non-therapy group. However, when I asked her if she would like to stop, she said, "Oh no, I'm fine. My therapist told me that this course would be good for me, and it is!" Tears turned into laughter as we identified with her story and her courage.

And then there was a participant who was very quiet for several days. He seemed preoccupied but did the writing assignments and shared his themes. I thought that he simply found the course boring and perhaps just needed to complete it to get the credit. Then one day, when we were sharing stories about our families and significant others, he told a story about his grandfather with whom he had been very close. The next day he looked as if a huge load had been lifted off his shoulders. He told me that he had been grieving the loss of his grandfather for a long time but did not realize it until he shared his story with us.

The lessons here are twofold: first, you have the ability to heal your spirit through letting go—in this case, in the form of telling your story—and second, there is healing power and meaning-value in simply getting the story out. You do not always need to understand everything or have an answer; sometimes stillness emerges simply by letting go. Healing occurs through reconnecting with your story. *Storytelling* keeps the journey to life going to the next destination, even if it is after a long layover. It is never too late.

My career in gerontology has been a priceless gift in learning about stillness in suffering and loss. Over the years, *storylistening*, observing, and working with older persons has assisted me in seeing that whatever happens in life, the journey can go on and there is always new life, if you can just be open to it. One example is my friend George Wakeling, whom you will meet in several chapters in this book. When I was at a very lonely period, he said that I should take a cruise. The reason, he said, is that he met his first wife on a cruise. After many years of marriage, she died. After some time, he took another cruise and met his second wife.

I have yet to take a cruise, but the message got through to me about being open to what may be out there. In fact, George's journey continued for a time, even after his second wife passed. He used to tell me that after you have been around the block a few times (as he had, at age ninety-three), you learn to see that things do move on and get better after bad times. He used to say that you have to learn to live with some chaos in your life. Perhaps you can find solace in the view that if anything is guaranteed in life it is change, even though it gives and takes away. Still, if you continue to learn and live with change, then perhaps it is a journey *to life*. Perhaps you can find the underlying stillness to it all.

CHAPTER 3
Your Life as a Story

BEING able to see your life as a story can be very helpful, healing, and freeing in many circumstances. Nevertheless, it is a process that is effective only over time. What I mean is that when you are in the middle of the storm, you are so busy *living* the story and being overwhelmed by what is happening that you cannot see the story from a distance; you cannot see the experience as a story.

I remember becoming very angry with a couple of well-meaning acquaintances who, early on in my suffering described in the Divorce and New Life chapter, would say, "Oh, you will be okay; you will find someone new and have a new chapter in your life," or, "Gee, I got divorced, and it did not do that to me!" This is not helpful when one is in great pain. It's far better to say nothing and simply be with the hurting individual, or say, "You must feel pretty bad right now."

However, once the worst of the pain starts to subside a little, and then over a longer period (and perhaps with the help of some relax-into-stillness movements), you may be able to see the experience from a bit of a distance—that is, as a story. One way is to apply story concepts to your life. One of these concepts is *genre*. For example, at first there was no story to tell in the Divorce and New Life chapter; there was just pain and confusion. But a bit later I began to feel that I was living a *tragic* story: the whole thing was a great personal tragedy, in my thoughts (hard done by, cruel world), feelings (the victim, how could she do this to me?), and actions (sad, not open to new relations).

Still later, the story became more like a *satire*, with sarcasm and irony (she even took the keys to the tractor. I hope she finds someone just like her!). This indicates some measure of letting go, of the possibility of space and stillness, and perhaps the beginning of a new story. I began to feel better with the support of good friends, but also by allowing stillness into my life. I began to let go and allow things to happen. I stopped trying to fix the situation, and I also realized that I could not do this alone.

(With regard to trying to fix things: I remember a wise counsellor who interrupted me as I continued to talk and talk about my problems. She asked, "Do you really need answers to all these questions?" This silenced and shocked me for a moment, and then I said, "No!" I felt very relieved after this session.)

After still more time, my experience became almost a *comedy*—at least an absurd, existential comedy ("Always look on the bright side of life," as Monty Python might say).

In my case, there are two more genres to mention. First, in the end the tragedy become a *romantic* and family story with a new partner and two teenage daughters. This was completely unexpected at the time, but I was open to see where the new path was heading.

Finally, the divorce was for me, in the end, an *ordinary wisdom* story and a spiritual experience that brought many valuable lessons. These lessons gave me an appreciation of, and much greater sensitivity to, the suffering of others. I also learned that there is no one way to grieve or to find stillness and new meaning in life. Additionally, I became very aware of the need for stillness in my life. Another great benefit of this experience was (and still is) that, as an academic, my theoretical understanding deepened and has been infused with an existential, or real-life dimension. I began to think and speak more from experience, and not only from book learning. Also, my martial arts training improved, partly because I began to understand that it is okay and even necessary to learn to fail or lose. Time often does heal, and it can be helped with a stillness perspective.

Explore your Pathway

Is there an event in your life for which you might entertain a *re-genre-ation*? Could this be a useful way to understand and bring more stillness to your own situation, or help someone you love? You only need to be willing to allow the experience to move from genre to genre as part of your journey. One way to work with this process is to relax into stillness and then write a short story of the event: first as a tragedy, then as a satire, followed by a comedy. Finally, without forcing, see if you can identify an ordinary wisdom story that emerges from your reflections on this experience.

CHAPTER 4
Time Is Not What You Think

YOU may take it for granted that time is one thing, which is a line that goes in one direction, from past to present to future. But if you look more closely, you may see that this is only one kind of time. And, in fact, in a way, there is no time. Also, the way you *live time* is very closely related to your experiences, to your own life story. It is true that you need to respect and understand time as it appears on a clock or a calendar—that is, outer, or clock time. Many aspects of your life are influenced by clock time: voting age, work and retirement issues, being able to have a drink legally, being eligible for discounts, and so on.

However, when it comes to many other age-related matters, an interesting question to ask yourself is, "How old would you be if you did not know how old you are?" I am past sixty-five years of age, which means that I am eligible for a pension mistakenly called *old age security* in Canada. But, as mandatory retirement was recently put to rest, I plan to remain in full-time employment for some time to come. My wife and I recently bought a new house, and according to the bank we could have a mortgage until I am eighty years old.

In the past this may have seemed totally unrealistic; however, as a gerontologist I know that we are now living into our eighties, nineties, and beyond, and most of us are not in a nursing home.

As the mortgage example shows, even outer time, coupled with the view of aging as change, can become more flexible or workable when looked at from the point of view of MAT (Meaning, Attitude, and Technology). However, you also experience other kinds of time. The only form of time that really exists is the present moment. Clock time is a human creation. You may notice that there are many *times* that you experience when there is no past or future—for example, when you have a romantic encounter and the minutes seem to go by timelessly. Or when you are waiting for the result of a test from the doctor, time seems to take forever. Time is different when you are in nature, playing a musical instrument, or engaged in other creative activities.

Researchers have found other examples. When people are asked to tell their life stories, they often say, "Where shall I begin?" The researcher says, "Begin wherever you want." Very often a person will start with a major life event, such as a marriage, birth of a child, or death of a spouse. This means that you experience time not only in a straight line, but on the basis of what is meaningful to you. Other researchers have found that those whom gerontologists call the oldest old group (more than eighty-five years of age) often feel that they live in a timeless present. What these examples show is that you do experience more than clock time. The next step is to realize that it is possible to make more time for *present-moment time* in your life. Stillness is found in the present moment when your monkey mind is not running the show. By finding ways to relax into stillness, you can experience more peace, and you can then be more flexible and creative in dealing with your clock-time story. Your past and your future can be given new meaning in the present moment.

Explore your Pathway

Think about your own experiences when you have been *out of time*. There is no past or future. Are there areas of your life where you could be more in present time? For example, my daughter has discovered that time stops when she is present and genuinely listening to another person's story. If you wish, try to identify three ideas and actions that could help time stop for you, and in this way invite more stillness into your life?

CHAPTER 5
Restorying Your Life

YOU grow, learn, and find meaning, ordinary wisdom, and stillness through stillness practice and through your life story. However, the restorying journey does not involve simply choosing a better story to replace the old one. Also, new meaning does not come from forcing yourself to think positively about a troublesome situation. In fact, I agree with the statement that *positive thinking* can become a prison.

Your life as a story is made up of thoughts, emotions, and actions or behaviour—that is, how you think, feel, and act. It may be possible to change your thoughts about something, and there are techniques to help you try this approach.

Yes, positive thinking is one of these techniques. However, the effort it takes to maintain this attitude may become exhausting, as with such challenges as chronic pain, for example, or an addiction. The problem is that you are still attempting to control or fix the problem, as your thinking mind scrambles around to find a *positive* solution. In addition to this, it is a prison in the sense that you are either a winner or a loser, depending on how successful you are in keeping up the program. In contrast to this, a stillness approach, such as restorying, suggests that you first get out of your thinking mind, step back, and try to see the larger picture.

In this way, instead of fighting or denying the particular change that has occurred in your life, you make room in your present story for the change that has occurred, or that you want to occur. It is about finding new meaning in your *whole* story, not just attempting to fix the broken part. While there are no guarantees, lasting change and stillness are more likely to occur in your life by following this approach. This is because you are hoping to change your entire story, which, again, includes how you think, feel, and act. Researchers who work with life stories—what is also called *narrative research*—have discovered that any change that occurs in one part of your life affects your entire life. This is true for chronic pain, widowhood, stroke, dementia, terminal illness, frailty, disability, and many other changes.

Increasingly, stillness approaches are also being used in substance abuse programs as they have the potential to help addicts to step outside the vortex of their *addiction story* by creating a space between their thoughts of using and their sensations and actions. In this way, you feel better about things by first giving yourself a break and connecting with your stillness. You do not split yourself between what you accept as "you" and the "you" that you do not want to accept. It is *all* you—the stillness and the area of suffering. For example, one of my colleagues works with people who suffer from depression. His clients at first say, "I am a depressed person." He tries to help them move to a different story: "I am a person who is experiencing depression."

In this way, there is less danger for the pain part of your story to take you over and run the show, because the pain story gets placed into the bigger story. At this point, there is a possibility that your ordinary wisdom can emerge and help you to find meaning, peace, and stillness, even in your suffering. You may not necessarily be happy, but you can find peace. I believe that this is what Buddhists mean when they say that you create your own world.

For example, what if you lose something or someone that means a great deal to you—say, a job or a relationship? You can easily become resentful, angry, and bitter—a victim. You may know someone who never moves beyond this attitude; it becomes for them a way of life, an identity as The Bitter One. In this way, you have created a hell realm for yourself, in the here and now. However, if you can accept the loss and the pain and no longer resist and try to control the situation, you may find that things get easier and better for you.

In a rather ironic way, losing and accepting bring a gaining of stillness and peace. That is because you are not letting go into nothing, but into stillness, which is no-thing, a comforting presence. It takes courage to let go. More often it seems that you let go out of exhaustion or desperation; you feel that you have tried everything else. Eckhart Tolle says that most of us are dragged, kicking and screaming, to enlightenment. I believe what he means is that we are all in stillness anyway, but until we learn to be better at letting go, our journey to stillness can be rough.

From this point of view, when things happen to you that you experience as loss and suffering, you are in fact being given an opportunity to connect with your stillness, and, in the end, to be free of suffering. I hardly need to add that this is easier said than done. Nevertheless, the practice of relaxing into stillness is designed precisely to help you on this journey to life, by responding to your suffering in a kinder and gentler way. Borrowing from the American Buddhist teacher Surya Das, you can move from having a *Velcro* mind, where thoughts and emotions stick to you, to a *Teflon* mind, where things move on and can be redirected to more stillness.

Explore your Pathway

Is there a change occurring in your life to which you might apply these restorying insights? Give yourself permission to relax into stillness, let go, and allow the change to become *one* part of your pathway, and of who you are.

CHAPTER 6
Finding Your Way

I invite you to continue to look at your life as a story, this time by exploring the *themes* that make your life meaningful to you. The more meaning, the more stillness.

To prime the pump, as my mentor, Jim Birren, would say, here are some common station stops on the journey. (I am also grateful to my friend and colleague Gary Reker for his important work on the concept of personal meaning.)

- *Significant others* (you may wish to consider family members, and significant others who are here, as well as those who have died. As I heard someone say recently, as long as I am around, they are still here.)
- *Friends*
- *Health*
- *Legacy/generativity* (the desire to leave something behind for future generations, making the world a better place, whether in the form of service, knowledge, mentorship, or other.)
- *Work/career*
- *Altruism/service to others*

- *Religion/spirituality*
- *Wisdom figures* (those who inspire you
  to seek meaning and stillness)
- *Learning/creativity*
- *The "good life"/adventure*
- *Others* (You may find meaning in unique ways, such
  as gardening, special collections, biking, or sitting
  by the sea. Possibly you have a hobby that is *more*
  in the sense that it gets you up in the morning with
  a purpose or allows you to have fun, or both. My
  ongoing barista training provides that for me.)

Sketching out your story

1. ***Using pen and paper, list the themes that are especially
   meaningful for your journey.*** By reflecting on and linger-
   ing with your list, you might want to celebrate and renew
   your connection with some of these sources of meaning.
   You may be pleasantly surprised at what comes up. You
   may wish to renew your marriage at the empty-nest stage.
   A priest friend went through a major crisis of meaning
   in his life. He eventually discovered that caring for his
   parishioners was a major source of meaning for him, and
   he found new meaning and stillness in this realization.

2. ***Ask yourself if there are some themes in your story that
   are more important than others.*** You may want to try to
   order the list as to which themes may have more meaning for
   you and which themes are not so significant. For example,
   is your work more important than your spiritual practice?

Does family come before friends? Or are there several themes that are equally meaningful to you? The reason for this second step is that in times of change you may use your list to give new direction on your journey. You can ask yourself if you would be able to let go of a source of meaning, or give it less importance, either if you had to or because you want to make different choices in your life.

3. *Allow yourself to explore new themes you could add to the list.* Use your imagination and *fantasize,* as my psychoanalyst friend Willi would say, and thus possibly discover a new source of meaning and stillness in your story. What if you lose your job or retire from your career? Take a look at your list and try to focus on what you have rather than on what you have lost. As my wife, Liz, says, think of yourself as eighteen again, with all the potentials and possibilities ahead of you, and play with that thought. Is there a person you left behind earlier in your journey? Perhaps you can renew, or place more emphasis on, friends and family, or be of service with your skills and experience—or do something completely different, perhaps something you have always wanted to do.

Here are some examples of fellow travellers who continue to explore their pathways to stillness:

- A former student spent his career as a social worker. He told me that he was retiring and that he always loved to cook. He has since completed a chef's course and recently opened a restaurant.

- My friend Daniel spent his career as a physicist and worked on the Hubble Space Telescope. At age seventy-six he returned to art school and completed a degree in fine arts. He then moved from the southern United States to Atlantic Canada, where he is now a sculptor and painter.
- A career radio personality in our area recently announced his retirement. A long-time musician, he planned to become a wandering minstrel.
- My friend Willi, who trained as a violinist fifty years ago, recently began playing again in an orchestra. He told me that performing again was a big surprise to him.
- My wife retired several years ago from a government job, where she worked in a cubicle all day. This job was very stressful for Liz as she is such a people person. She now operates a bed and breakfast. In this new setting she gives full expression to her gift of making people feel rested and nurtured—something the guests express again and again. This is a major source of meaning in her life. (She even manages to achieve this in spite of the occasionally question-able quality of labour from her assistant—namely, me!)
- Another former student of mine lost her husband. After some time she returned to university, completed an arts degree and is now a volunteer with hospice.

I would like to emphasize that the stories of those who have found new meaning should not be taken as examples of *successful* aging. This journey is about *meaningful* aging; the "success" comes from being willing to show up, not from the outcome of the activity. The word *success* implies that you can fail, whereas with *meaning* there are no winners and losers, just creating and discovering. Stillness comes from following where you seem to be led, not whether what you do works out or not.

Reflecting on the sources of meaning in your life can be helpful throughout your journey. As the saying goes, aging is not for sissies. Just think of all the changes you have been through in mind, body, and spirit—some wonderful, some not so much. Growing older can be a particular challenge to women in that you may need to seek new sources of meaning after being a daughter, wife and/or mother, and perhaps not having taken time for *you*.

Finally, an important source of meaning can be that you simply value and even celebrate that you have managed to survive this far on the journey. As someone said, at times it takes courage to just be on this planet. Relaxing into stillness and being open to what is meaningful to you can help you avoid possible depression and despair, and guide you to more stillness.

Explore your Pathway

Think about experiences in your life that you can say that you survived. It may not be a big thing to others, but for you it may be a source of meaning and stillness. For example, some participants in my guided autobiography groups start out by saying that they really do not have much of a life story to tell, since they were just a housewife—that is, until they look more closely! After reviewing her experiences: raising four children, schooling, illness, activities, managing a household, and being a wife to her husband, one participant said that she did not know how she did it. She said that although science tells us that we cannot do two things at once, mothers can indeed do this. By relaxing into stillness and gently exploring your journey, you may find much unique meaning-value and the stillness associated with that discovery.

CHAPTER 7
Aging is a Journey, Not a Problem

THERE is a huge divide between the very powerful negative stereotypes of aging in the *outer* public domain and your actual *inner* experiences and attitudes as an older person. If you look only at the outside of aging, you may become old before your time, simply by believing in what are, in reality, *ageist* stereotypes, which are not based on facts, but myths. They are unreflected, taken-for-granted beliefs. Your employer may look at you as an older worker and think that you are no longer competent because of your age, when the employer is the same chronological age. Curious that they think they are doing a good job themselves! Mandatory retirement, now thankfully almost defunct in Canada and many other countries, is both an outcome and a cause of these ageist attitudes. As an acquaintance told me, "Did something happen to me during the night? Because I woke up this morning and was sixty-five and not sixty-four, and today I do not have my job to go to."

As you grow older, you may have a tendency to attribute things simply to aging and being older—that is, according to clock time and outer aging. Many health professionals still interact with patients in this way. A concise way to illustrate this is with the story of an eighty-year-old man who goes to the doctor with a problem in his left knee. The doctor says, "What do you expect at your age?" The man responds that his right knee is the same age and it is fine! The doctor automatically and mistakenly assumes that you will be frail and in decline once you are older.

There is also a danger that, if you buy into the negative stereotypes that are imposed from the outside, you can become an object to others and perhaps even to yourself. Nowhere is this more tragic than in residential care settings and hospitals. While this situation is gradually improving, it remains a serious problem, and, as with the earlier example, reflects a lack of training in sound gerontological principles among professionals and families. I refer here to the tendency to address older persons, "How are *we* today, dear?" This form of address is both objectifying and condescending.

What, then, is aging, if viewed from the inside? Aging, in part, includes changes that take place throughout the journey to life, and to which MAT (Meaning, Attitude, Technology) can be applied. Many of these changes are losses—relationships, physical abilities, careers, even beliefs that had meaning and no longer make sense.

Isn't it interesting that, no matter your age, there is no calendar time in which you feel yourself to be old *all of a sudden?* A nun eighty-five years of age once told me that she cares for the "old" nuns in her convent. Being "old" has very little to do with chronological aging and a lot to do with frailty. If you become ill, you may start to consider yourself old at some point. Otherwise, as researchers have discovered, you do not have an age identity. If asked, many older persons will say that, inside, they feel that they are like they were in their thirties or forties. The popular saying, "You're as old as you feel," captures this sentiment, as does "Aging is in your mind."

The term "old" refers to the outside story of aging—how you are perceived and treated by others. The word "disabled"—or, more correctly, persons with special abilities—echoes this view in stating that the most difficult challenge of their special abilities is dealing with how others relate to them, not the disability itself.

Even if you look at the outside evidence of aging, there are many changing abilities that can be compensated for, and maintained far into the physical journey, by MAT. This means that some of these changes are facilitated by technology, some by medications, some by physical activity programs. However, the key to the effectiveness of these interventions is your willingness to embrace the journey as a pathway to stillness, rather than giving up at the first sign of a fall from the heights.

Explore your Pathway

Try a "relax into stillness" movement at the end of the book. Then ask yourself how you might see your present aging as a journey or story of ongoing changes? Try to shift your focus from outer aging to inner aging. How could MAT be helpful here?

CHAPTER 8
It All Depends on How You Look at It

I have acquaintances and friends who struggle with issues such as the need for hearing aids and eyeglasses. They feel that once they begin to need these kinds of support, they are old and will die soon. And many of us feel this uncomfortable sense of aging and mortality when we think about writing a will or advance directive. This is the power of the negative stereotypes of aging.

Another example involves the use of canes. Many of us would benefit and experience greater independence if we availed ourselves of this form of assistance, but we do not want to appear old or disabled, so we attach a negative story to this experience. Yet I noticed in Europe that many people own unique and fashionable walking sticks; I have seen many older persons hiking in the Alps with the assistance of these devices. In fact, hiking sticks are now quite popular everywhere. Again, it's all about the perception and significance attached to a common age-related phenomenon. The problem is not necessarily with the change but with your story of the change—its meaning, your attitude, and your willingness to embrace technological advances. Again, MAT (Meaning, Attitude, and Technology) is key.

My friend George Wakeling exemplified living by the MAT concept. When I met George he had just moved to Fredericton, New Brunswick, and he immediately wanted to connect with the community, St. Thomas University, and our gerontology program. He was eighty years old at the time, and was very instrumental in helping us establish the Third Age Centre, a centre run by and for older adults in the community. For the next fourteen years, until his death at age ninety-four, we were good friends and worked on many projects together. He also practised some light-hearted *reverse ageism* on me. Here are three examples:

First, when they were less common, George already had a scanner and was up on the latest computer programs. He used to ask me why I did not know about these things since I was a professor. Second, he had a full head of hair his entire life, and he used to point to his head and say, "See, I am much older than you and you have no hair." And third, he did not require corrected vision; he would say, "I can see without glasses and you cannot."

George was very independent for ninety years of his life, but when the time came, he was willing to accept help from others. When he no longer felt safe driving his car, I would take him shopping at the supermarket, This in itself was a major transition for him, and he found the wisdom to accept this change in attitude. When we went shopping, at first he would not let me push the cart through the store—but later he asked me to push the cart. However, if I tried to get something from the shelf for him, he would say, "No,

I can do that myself." After more time passed, he began to ask me to get the product from the shelf for him.

I recall when he was invited to a wedding in England, his original home. He said he would not go because he could not make the long walk through Pearson Airport in Toronto. I encouraged him to take the transportation service available to him within the airport. He said that he did not want to be one of those "old fogeys" riding in the cart. I told him that he had a right to the service and that many VIPs ride those carts to the gate—movie stars, prime ministers, royalty. He thought about it, and the next day he said he was going to the wedding. He was able to find new meaning inside for his situation, and thus could continue on his journey.

George's story shows what can happen if you are willing to calm down and be open to looking at aging as changing in a different way. It may be possible to change the story—to *restory* a situation—by finding new meaning, a new attitude, or by using available technology. In this way, you may retain or bring more stillness and peace to your life.

Explore your Pathway

As in the previous chapter, continue to you see your present stage of aging as a journey or story of ongoing changes and shift your focus from outer aging to inner aging. How could MAT (Meaning, Attitude, and Technology) be helpful to you and to those around you, regardless of age?

CHAPTER 9

The Outside is Different from the Inside

THERE are more serious changes that can occur on the journey of aging, such as dementia. For those who experience this, either directly or in proximity to a loved one, it can be hard to encounter the common belief that nothing can be done for these travellers, except to feed and house them. It can feel like an immediate death sentence, as if the journey is over.

However, this is far from the truth. Medications can now maintain a person's level of functioning for years. And, even as the disease progresses, environmental and interpersonal interventions can assist you to maintain dignity and communication long into the disease. No one would dispute that dementia is an insidious and devastating condition. However, need it end my journey or the journey of a loved one, or someone in my care as a fellow traveller? The following example illustrates the contrast between an outside view of this kind of change and the inside view of aging as a journey to life.

At Christmas some years ago, I went to Montreal to visit my aunt Mary, who was living in a special care home. At one point during the visit, I asked the owner of the home if we could take a photo of my aunt near the Christmas tree in the living room. But near the tree was an older lady sitting in a wheelchair with her head down, working her fingers with some wool that was wrapped around the arm of the wheelchair.

"Oh, just move her away," said the owner. "She's crazy and doesn't know where she is or what she is doing."

Out of respect for this lady, I approached her and asked if it was okay to move her. When there was no response, we did so. We took our pictures with my aunt and eventually completed our visit. When I was leaving I decided to wish all the residents a Merry Christmas and shake their hands. I approached the woman we had relocated from the tree, offered my hand, and said, "Merry Christmas to you." She looked up into my eyes and clearly said, "The same to you and to your family."

I left the home almost in tears and in a moral quandary. I wondered if I should tell the owner that she did not know how to care for these travellers. *Will that help*, I asked myself, *or will it result in worse care for both my aunt and the older person by the tree?* This woman was in a setting that made it difficult to find her journey to life with a measure of stillness and peace, as she was being treated from an outside, ageist perspective.

This encounter with the lady by the Christmas tree showed me that when we encounter others in this way—looking at the inside rather than just the outside—our own journey is affirmed by life as well. As the spiritual teacher Jean Vanier once said, you begin by thinking that you are helping others, and you realize later that they are a gift to you.

Bob and Leo

Early dementia survivors (as opposed to victims) show us how it is possible to find meaning in the face of severe challenges on the journey to life. Here are two examples:

Bob was a guest lecturer in my Introduction to Gerontology class. After having survived the shock of diagnosis and early problems with medication, he began to volunteer through the local Alzheimer Society and give public talks. He told us that he had never given a public talk until he was diagnosed with the disease. As you can imagine, after listening to this gentleman there was not a dry eye in the room.

The second example is a colleague at St. Thomas University. Leo, until his recent death, was a retired professor emeritus in the philosophy department. He was diagnosed with Alzheimer's disease. Following his diagnosis, he guest lectured in my gerontology class on two occasions. His favourite story about the disease was that he was able to deny it for quite a while by claiming to be an absent-minded professor. This is both true and an example of the humour he brought to his situation. He eventually wrote a book with his partner about his illness experiences. He said that at first it was incredible, but hard things take time to be fully accepted. He pointed out that we can also have a tendency to save face by keeping silent about unfortunate things that happen to us. We want to keep them hidden, he explained, yet once we accept the truth, there is nothing to hide, and we are free. Leo told me that the diagnosis of Alzheimer's disease eventually gave him new meaning and purpose in life—to help others deal with the disease through writing, speaking, and being a survivor. Leo was also a student in my Tai Chi class at York Care Centre. This letting go and acceptance brought a measure of stillness to Leo's life under very challenging circumstances, as it did with Bob.

Explore your Pathway

If you wish, try a relax-into-stillness movement the end of the book. Then take a look at your personal and/or professional life. Are there situations or relationships where you could move from an outside to an inside story perspective. By storylistening you may move beyond "storyotyping" another person, or yourself, and thus enrich your journey with meaning and stillness.

CHAPTER 10
Meaningful Aging—Max

MAX was a friend of mine who died recently; he was in his late seventies. He was a very macho man who had loved contact sports all his life. He played rugby, was a martial artist, and walked the Santiago de Compostela trail on his seventieth birthday. As he entered his seventies, things changed. He became seriously ill for a time, and his wife, whom he loved dearly, died. We trained at the same Tai Chi school, but now he had severe balance problems, and was grieving as well. He did two things that he said helped him at this time. First, he decided he would not refuse any invitation to go out with friends, or anyone else for that matter. Second, he asked me to come to his home on a regular basis and teach him Tai Chi.

We began by training in the usual way—that is, standing—but eventually I suggested that we had better do seated Tai Chi, a special programme that I developed some years ago. Max resisted this as he loved to ask me to show him the self-defence applications of the moves. As I said, he was macho. However, he gradually let go, accepted, gave up control, and we practised the seated version. I helped him give in to this change by reminding him that Tai Chi is about breathing, relaxing, and stillness.

As time passed, we would practise on his back deck in the sun, watching the birds, and with his dog observing. He would often remark how peaceful he felt and that it was a little paradise. I am sure that this stillness practice did not take away the challenges of his physical changes, nor did it remove the sadness of losing his wife. However, it gave him moments of peace and something meaningful to look forward to on a regular basis. In other words, it was a pathway to stillness.

Explore your Pathway

Is there an area of your life where you might consider following Max in accepting, letting go, and possibly finding new meaning and stillness through personal loss?

CHAPTER 11
Stillness in Giving—and in Self-Care

I hear many stories in both my personal and professional life about those who try to do the right thing, help others, and be of service. Is there a better or worse way for us to do this? I am guided by the insights of several wisdom figures who have devoted their lives to others. These include Henri Nouwen, the Dalai Lama, and Jean Vanier. These teachers suggest that being of service is best carried out from a place of abundance and peace in your heart. In contrast, helping others from a place of guilt, exhaustion, or a fearful attempt to save a broken world may not serve you or others well. I once heard the Dalai Lama say that he was a very selfish person because helping others out of love gave him so much pleasure.

Recently, my priest friend Bill told me that some time ago, after many decades in his vocation, he came to the realization that God does not need him to be a priest. The experience was very disillusioning, and it caused him to seriously question what he was doing. However, he eventually came to the realization that caring for his congregation as a priest brought him the most meaning in his life, compared to other possible paths.

Jim, another friend of mine, was a minister for twenty years. He also said that he came to see that God did not need him to be a minister. Jim left the ministry because this insight freed him from a lifestyle that did not give him meaning any longer.

These friends experienced a shift from the outside story to the inside story. Both these friends continue to serve and love others, but from a place of stillness, freedom, and personal meaning—not from an exterior source of motivation. Helping others includes helping yourself and being true to yourself. More than this, caring for yourself *is* part of caring for others. If you do not care for yourself, everyone suffers.

A common contemporary social phenomenon is that of adult children moving back home. In my circle, there are parents who enjoy this arrangement. However, most of them feel that, although they would like to help their children, they do not really like them back under the same roof. They often tell me that the children do not help out with housework, cooking, or the finances.

These parents feel that they would prefer freedom; they've been there, done that. They experience anxiety and resentment, but feel stuck. In these cases, the service to the children is perhaps not achieving the goal of the larger picture. They may be forgetting that the purpose of raising children is to free them to seek and discover their own wisdom and stillness. I have good friends in Germany who made their decision in this way. They told their children, "Once you leave home, it is now our time as a couple and we will be moving to a small place. We will help you as we can, but you will not be living here anymore." They continue to have a very loving relationship with their children, but they also have their own freedom.

Even from a financial perspective, you may find that an adult child does not wish to accept a particular kind of work to at least temporarily help their cause. You may wish to reflect on your own story and how you managed to provide for your children in earlier years. As my wife and I often say, those efforts and uncertain times bring much meaning and sense of purpose to your life. Are you preventing your children from having that opportunity? Are you inadvertently keeping all parties from experiencing more meaning and stillness?

I once heard an interview with a well-known social activist. The interviewer asked if he thought any of his work actually made a difference in the world. The activist explained that for him there was an inside story of service and an outside story. The outside story is, in the end, out of his control. Sometimes things change and often they do not, at least not in the short term. However, the inside story is that he feels that his work is a spiritual practice and that it is a major source of meaning and serenity in his life. He does not need the outside to meet his expectations in order to make the inside worthwhile. To me, this also means that being a martyr to a cause is not the only path to pursue.

Stillness brings more space and choices to a situation, resulting in creative solutions that are not knowable in advance. You need not necessarily feel locked in or trapped in a caregiving situation. It is possible that guilt may prevent you from seeing choices that are healthier for you, as well as for the person for whom you are caring.

Stillness practice can help you find meaningful options; it can bring still more stillness as a result of better outcomes for all concerned in this biographical encounter. Your story counts, too!

My friend Ardeth has developed a test in which she asks herself if she is being a cheerful giver in a particular situation. If not, she revisits the situation. You may find it interesting that there is a transition occurring in the professions from the use of the term *caregiver* to *care partner.* The idea of partner implies choice and empowerment for both characters in the story of compassionate care.

Give yourself some freedom to choose. You do not need to be controlled by the expectations of others. As difficult as it may be to make this transition, loving with detachment is real love.

Sometimes you may end up doing the same things, but if it is a choice and not a victim scenario, it will have more meaning and stillness for you. Stillness practice can help you let go and give *in* to your situation, which is not giving *up* or resigning yourself to your fate. The journey remains open and the story can continue toward a better destination, a new chapter.

Many caregivers of those with dementia become ill and die before their loved ones. Instead of fear and exhaustion, why not try to bring stillness to this part of your journey, seek out resources that can give you a break, alter your home to make it more accessible and comfortable? At the Wu's Tai Chi school where I train, there is a student who comes to class regularly. She is a care partner with her husband at home. She says the classes give her a break; she finds stillness in the practice, and also feels support from the camaraderie of others in the class. It gives her a sense of normalcy, which she says is necessary to her wellbeing and life.

Explore your Pathway

Life is complicated and there are no quick answers, but a useful guideline is the following: Does the decision you are making bring more stillness to you and to those you care for, or less? Can you think of ways in which the shift from care *giving* to *partnering* could allow you both to find meaning, ordinary wisdom, and stillness in your situation?

CHAPTER 12
Loneliness

DEALING with the pain of loneliness is not easy, and as much as we'd like to avoid it entirely, we have no choice but to experience it. We can learn much from loneliness and other forms of suffering, but there needs to be a balance in our approach to this part of our journey.

When I was younger, I enjoyed good wine and beer; drinking was a comfort behaviour to remedy loneliness. At some point, I somehow resolved that, before I would get drunk, I would have an intense martial art workout. I would wrap a blanket around a tree in my yard and kick and punch it for an hour. I told myself that if I still wanted a drink after that, I would go ahead. And I usually did still have energy to drink. But I always felt that something healthy was also happening because of this routine.

These days, drinking is not a main comfort behaviour for me. Now I follow a practice that Eckhart Tolle speaks about. I first sit with the feelings and allow the questions and pain to be there without attempting to find an answer or even to understand what is going on. If this is not possible, I try to accept that I cannot sit with it. I do this for a time, and then phone a friend, watch television, eat something, do some relax-into-stillness movements—you get the idea. Little by little, this practice has resulted in more feelings of solitude and stillness instead of raw loneliness, although loneliness still happens at times. I believe that to the extent we can do this practice, we feel free inside and free to be with others in a less needy way. We experience less striving and more stillness, which includes a sense of having nothing to do and nowhere to go.

There can be a measure of peace from either of these attitudes— accepting the pain or accepting that we cannot accept it. This is in contrast to longing for the past or hoping too much in the future, which can cause more pain and cause us to overlook a new insight or miss what is present now. There are many questions that we ask ourselves when we are lonely: *Why do I feel this way? Why can't I do something to fix this? What did I do to deserve this? What is going to happen to me?* These questions are natural; I do not believe you can prevent them from arising.

However, what you can do—instead of getting caught up in the noise of these questions—is to try to sit still and *watch the movie.* In other words, try to observe the pain and the questions as they travel past your consciousness. Let things happen without creating a story about them all.

Also, there are different forms of loneliness. One form arises when we miss a significant other, which could be a child, a parent, a lover, or a good friend. Another kind of loneliness comes from any experience of loss, whether through illness, the ending of a career, or any other kind of trauma. In these circumstances we feel separate and alone—from other people, from our community, and even from God. This experience of loneliness can be very intense and can make us feel totally abandoned—that we have lost our story. This radical form of loneliness often occurs in situations of bereavement overload, which means that unpleasant experiences sometimes seem to come all at once. When it rains, it pours.

Then there is existential loneliness. Even though we may be with those who love us, from time to time there can still arise a sense of utter loneliness. This kind of loneliness just happens, and we cannot attribute it to anything in particular. In many cases, this kind of loneliness may be the result of a crisis of meaning in our life. There is nothing wrong in particular, but as Bill, a priest friend who grew up on a farm, describes it, in these moments we are being called to a time of planting seeds. Seeds are planted underground and in the dark. They incubate and then reach out to the light and to new life. Butterflies are another wonderful metaphor for this process. However, during the underground period, we may be inside and not as *available* as usual. It is healthy to give yourself permission to experience this part of your journey and to rely on the understanding of loved ones, as it will most likely result in more stillness and presence to others.

Thankfully, the journey of loneliness is a necessary but not sufficient condition of being human. We can try to see loneliness in a different way—to view it as part of the journey, to be aware of what there is to see in it rather than as something to be denied and avoided. We cannot solve loneliness, but perhaps we can find meaning in it. Again, loneliness can turn into solitude if we try to be open to the journey. I find that I feel lonely not only because I am alone, but also because I feel separate from others and the world. At other times I feel alone but at peace as I feel connected with the world around me and connected to loved ones, who need not be physically present. More solitude and less loneliness come from allowing myself to be lonely when it arises. Somehow, surrendering to this process little by little brings more solitude and stillness, and less suffering.

Paradoxically, loneliness can cause something that was preventing us from feeling more connected fall away. We may find that though we may not have chosen it, loneliness does us some good. Perhaps this is why a monk I know once said, "Solitude and silence give birth to love." The journey to life is more about letting things go and falling away than gaining and achieving. The alternative is to put ourselves at risk of *narrative foreclosure*—the premature closing off of our journey, which can mean a life of bitterness, isolation, and a lack of new meaning. We need to arrive at a point of basic trust that everyone is in pain and that we can share that pain and share the resulting peace that comes from a connected journey. For some, it feels safer to cling to what we have, even if it is destructive. Or we wait for the right thing or right person to come along, based on a story we tell ourselves, rather than being open to the journey right in front of us. Relax-into-stillness movements and stillness stories can help us arrive at a point of being willing to listen to what surrounds us.

Explore your Pathway

The next time you are lonely, give yourself permission to sit with the experience, even for a short time; at first it could be for a just a few minutes. Tell yourself that you do not need an immediate answer or solution to this feeling.

CHAPTER 13
Denial to Acceptance

WHEN things go wrong—and it could be any experience of major disappointment, illness, or trauma—we often first deny that it is happening. To do so is natural and even healthy, as it gives us a chance to have a space between us and the experience. Moreover, it is natural to resist something that will change the story of our life that we were living before the experience of major change, and which robs us of any stillness that we may have had. I have often observed the following pathway through loss, which is based on the work of Elizabeth Kübler-Ross, in my own life, and in the lives of others in listening to their stories. It is a pathway, and not a highway, in that you may experience these phases in your own way, and in your own time.

Denial, in the form of shock and disbelief, is the first response to major suffering. However, after some time, we may move from denial to anger. Anger is the point where we begin to dimly realize that something has happened, that our life will not be as it was before. Anger is an attempt to resist and maintain control. Our expectations have been betrayed. From this phase we move to bargaining. *Can I make a deal to reverse the outcome?* Ingmar Bergman's film *The Seventh Seal*, in which a knight plays chess with Death to win more time, is a classic example of this phase of the journey. (Or perhaps you would prefer Woody Allen's version in his play *Death Knocks*.) At the bargaining phase, we are still resisting, still looking for control.

It is only in the next phase of the journey, depression, that the beginnings of surrender, letting go, or yielding become evident. Depression, in this context, is not necessarily a clinical phenomenon; it is more akin to sadness. In this phase, we have a deeper realization that no amount of denial, anger, or bargaining will change what has happened. Our ability to keep fighting and to resist is exhausted.

It is only at this point that we begin to relinquish our old story and become open to the possibility of a new one—that is, to the restorying process. In Eckhart Tolle's words, "Surrender comes when you no longer ask, 'Why is this happening to me?'" We do not understand what is going on and we need to become comfortable with that lack of understanding. In my experience of over thirty years of working with students, older persons in the community, and professionals, I have found that, with few exceptions, we eventually reach the final phase of acceptance. Acceptance does not amount to unbridled euphoria, or even happiness. If you think about it, you can find stillness and peace without being happy. However, neither does it connote resignation, giving up, or abandoning yourself in despair. It is an experience of new meaning, even if you cannot give words to that experience. While it cannot be forced, acceptance of the unacceptable is perhaps the major pathway to stillness.

Explore your Pathway

Can you identify a situation in your life, past or present, where the above pathway through loss would help you make sense of what happened or is happening? If it concerns another person, can you observe, through *storylistening*, which step in the pathway they are on, and could this help you relate to them in a more understanding way? For example: If a loved one is in the anger phase, you might relax into stillness, and allow them to vent safely, which would in turn allow them to possibly move toward acceptance and more stillness. Or you may feel more comfortable with their silence if they are in the depression phase, or be more patient if you observe yourself in this phase.

CHAPTER 14
Your Life as a Journey

WHAT does it mean to say that human life is a journey? Is it possible for you to live your life as a journey, and if so, are there some helpful guidelines? Where is this journey going? What is the point of undertaking the journey in the first place? There are many other metaphors of life, some of which participants in my guided autobiography courses have expressed. These include life as a cactus patch, a flowing river, a branching tree, a pizza, or a mobile. We can create images that characterize our life. So, if you have a choice as to how to look at your life, why not try the journey?

There is something optimistic and hopeful contained within the metaphor of the journey. When you are going on a trip, there is much anticipation. I know I enjoy imagining the journey long before it occurs. One of my favourite destinations is Europe. Months before the actual trip, I take out my maps. I search the Internet for places to stay, look at train schedules, contact friends. For me, the process of the journey is as enjoyable as the destination. The image of a journey includes characteristics and feelings such as curiosity, wonder, openness, and discovery. You may notice that a central aspect of a journey involves transcending your previous limits, as well as a sense of presence or availability. You are ready to learn new things, to explore, to not be overly preoccupied and encumbered with your self and your issues.

You may also notice that, even if things do not go according to plan, it takes a major disruption to alter the positive feelings on a journey. Despite the possible occurrence of a bad trip, a journey is not usually a negative experience, even though difficulties may occur, such as bad weather, missed connections, illness, a severed relationship, or loneliness. The journey *to* your life is a particular kind of journey. Let's explore the features of this journey.

Your journey is personal

As human beings, we are all alike in some ways; some of us are alike in other ways; and none of us are alike in yet other ways.

But in the end, your journey is unique. You have a personal itinerary that differs from anyone else. You have your own set of past experiences, present perceptions, and future expectations. Beyond this, you also have and are a unique *inside story* of these experiences and expectations. I may have a similar experience to you, but it means something different to me. You perceive and understand the world, other persons, and yourself from a unique point of view.

You are not alone

The fact that you have your own personal journey, or inside story, does not mean that you are isolated and separate from everyone else. Your journey is deeply connected to the world around you and to other people. You are not alone! Your very being originates from the genetic material of your parents. You are dependent upon others early in life and in one way or another throughout life. Thich Nhat Hanh calls this *interbeing*.

As a human being, you share a common itinerary that includes birth, development, aging, and death. You also share "station stops" such as as schooling, marriage, raising a family, the empty nest, widowhood, and the many other forms of joy and suffering that characterize life on this planet. Whether you individually experience some of these stops or not, you have a relationship to them. For example, if you marry, you have one experience; if you do not marry, you still have a story about not being married, being divorced, widowed, or never married. In your shared social world, you find and create meaning by observing the journey of those around you. The same is true for money, sexuality, and so on.

From the point of view of the journey, as the Zen Buddhist saying goes, you are on your own, together with everything. This means that the human journey is both unique and shared at the same time. There is a part of your journey that is intensely unique, personal, and not knowable by another. Yet, by nature, you are not set off from others—quite the contrary. Our original state is that you and I are together in trust, presence, love, and communion, as many spiritual teachers remind us. You may decide to separate yourself from the shared journey; there are many forms of alienation, isolation, and narrative foreclosure (deciding to close down your story). In the Al-Anon tradition, this shutting down is attributed to a combination of self-pity, resentment, depression, and anger. You decide that your problem is so unique that no one could possibly understand you.

But even if you go out to others for help or insight on your journey, you must make the insight your own; it must have meaning for you—in your feelings, beliefs, and actions, and in what you feel, think, and do. You need to go *through* your own journey. You cannot do an end run, and simply take on another outside story, whether that be a religion, person, teacher, or partner. Much of the journey is finding your own meaning in the ordinary, and new insights in old truths, through *storytelling* and *storylistening*. You listen to another and then say, "I can use that in my own way." Ultimately, stillness is discovered in sharing your special journey with the world. Your journey is *our* journey.

The journey is partly hidden

Another important feature of our journey to life is that its landscape resembles a winding mountain path or a river rather than than a freeway or prairie highway. This means that the traveller cannot know everything in advance, or even in hindsight. It is just not possible for us to gain a completely clear, panoramic vision of the journey. We cannot see what will occur farther along the way or around the next bend. It is like there is intermittent fog on the trail. This means that our journey necessarily involves an element of chance, of risk. Things are often indeterminate and open-ended, not fixed. On the one hand, we need to make decisions and choices based on partially known, partially hidden circumstances; a pathway or tributary must be taken. Yet under these conditions we will make mistakes of omission and commission; things will happen, as Robbie Burns tells us, in the best laid plans of mice and men.

Opacity, risk, and the unknown are basic conditions of the journey to life. Risk and leaps are basic to our journey. To imagine otherwise will only result in disappointment and disillusionment. As human travellers, we live life first and understand it, if at all, only from looking back along the trail we have just traversed. We are not transparent to ourselves; nor are we able to read off the truth about reality and life as a basis for knowing what to do next. This unclear and limited way of seeing is part of our humanness.

Does the journey end?

The human traveller is finite. Death is an unavoidable station on the voyage, and, in one sense, it places a limit on the duration of my journey and yours. We die, and we know that we will die. As with the discussion of risk, it does not make sense to leave death out. Robert Kastenbaum, the pioneering gerontologist-thanatologist, writes that his books are not about death but about life with death left in. Similarly, the Tibetan Buddhist spiritual teacher Sogyal Rinpoche tells us that the title of the original *Tibetan Book of the Dead* is not completely accurate. It is for this reason that he entitled his book *The Tibetan Book of Living and Dying*.

Death is an integral part of the journey. However, since it is part of the opaqueness and indeterminacy of the journey that the nature of death is unknown to you, at least experientially, it is possible to view death as part of the voyage. This means that you may be able consider death as an open question, another aspect of the path.

Upon reflection, you may discover your own sense of what death means, and that meaning can change as you pass through the stations of the journey to life. Death may mean something different to you in youth, middle age, and at the end of life. Your personal story of death may change depending on your experiences. In my experience, based on research and conversations with older persons, dying persons, and practitioners who work with the terminally ill, death from the outside is very different from the way in which people actually feel about death and its meaning to them. On this topic, I would recommend David Kuhl's book *What Dying Patients Want.* In a nutshell, what dying people want is what we all want: acceptance, belonging, honesty—and, I would add, stillness.

Your death may be viewed, among other things, as a wall, as a door, or as an open question. My point is that your life can be viewed as a journey, but a journey that does not necessarily end as a fait accompli—that is, as a fact to which you simply have to resign yourself. It can have many meanings. Further, the journey is indefinite in duration because you do not know the time of your death. Finally, the indefiniteness of the duration of the journey is highlighted by the fact that death may end a life, but it need not end a relationship.

The death of someone close to you may provide one of the most potent opportunities or catalysts for wonder, openness, and a search for meaning and stillness. The loss of a fellow pilgrim does not remove the experience of what the person meant to you. You may find that a loved one who has died is still felt to be present and continues to share your journey in important ways. Recently, I went on a seven-day silent retreat. While sitting in a chair outside in the morning sun with my eyes closed, I distinctly felt my father's presence. He died sixteen years ago. He was an alcoholic, so I was angry with him even though he was a good father while I was growing up. In this "visit" I felt the anger release, and that we were close again. This experience has given me a stillness boost.

Impermanence of the traveller's experience

A final important feature of viewing your life as a journey is that it implies a dynamism, an ever-changing landscape, another destination. The journey to life is one of transition and movement. However, in agreement with Viktor Frankl, the transitory nature of our existence in no way makes it meaningless. The fact that your life is always on the move does not mean that the past is not meaningful to the present and the future. It does suggest, though, that standing still or being rigid is not part of being on a journey.

To summarize, the journey metaphor tells us that being human means being on the way or en route, to use the existentialist philosopher Gabriel Marcel's words. The journey you are on has five dimensions. First, it is personal and unique while, second, being interpersonal and shared. Third, it is opaque, because there are hidden or unknowable features. Fourth, your journey is indefinite in its duration, and, fifth, it is impermanent or transitory. Underlying these features of the journey is a quality of hopefulness or life affirmation that offers the possibility for meaning and stillness for the entire journey. All who wander are not lost.

Explore your Pathway

There is an existentialist saying that human life is a search for love and meaning in the face of death. You may be able to embrace a *lighter* view of change and "endings" by relaxing into stillness and by applying the metaphor of the journey to your life.

So take some time to explore your life as a journey. Can you think of a metaphor or image to describe your journey? Allow yourself to meander along your pathway with curiosity and even a sense of humour.

CHAPTER 15

So What Does This Journey Mean for Your Life?

AT first glance, many of the features of the journey to life just discussed would seem to provide an excellent opportunity to become depressed or to experience existential dizziness. To the thinking mind or ego, characteristics of impermanence, indefiniteness, and opacity do not provide a basis for stability, control, and predictability. We could easily imagine a better deal than constant change, an unknown limit, and many things we cannot understand or even have sufficient awareness to know. Yet change and non-transparency do not equal chaos. If we look at the metaphor closely, there are three guidelines that can enhance our ability to live your life as a journey.

First, it does not seem to matter ultimately *what* has happened in our lives, so long as we can say that we did and are doing our best under the circumstances of our journey. Mistakes are made, *stuff happens*, the wrong path is taken, and unexpected crises and even catastrophes occur. Nevertheless, as long as the voyage of life continues—as long as we can view it as a journey—there is a movement onward. Over time, it may be possible to understand all experience as transitory: the trip was what it was, is what it is, and it continues. The impermanence of everything leaves open the possibility to create and discover new meaning; to choose a new destination or itinerary; and to acknowledge, appreciate, and even celebrate what we have already experienced on our personal journey. We can learn to value ourselves as good travellers, sometimes by simply appreciating the fact that we have survived and are still here. Further, as discussed in other chapters in this book, telling the story of your journey to yourself and others is an excellent way to come to appreciate your own journey to life. In this sense, the journey metaphor makes life more fluid or workable—you are not locked in by life. The heaviness is not in things, but in you and me.

The second guideline is that we need to develop a healthy respect for the necessary opaqueness of the journey. We understand certain things, need to accept others, and wonder about many more. As the journey goes on, our vision of life is ever changing. Our lives, which by definition include the process of aging and the fact of death, cannot be completely controlled or mastered, solved, or resolved. The *mastered* approach presupposes an omnipotent point of view to which we as the travellers are not privy.

Our journey involves both taking action—an attitude with which we are more familiar—and being receptive. We cannot trust that the vision or the meaning will remain the same. Something we found very meaningful can change and lose its meaning, sometimes with little warning. Also, we cannot trust that we will see more or less than we saw the previous time we were at a similar station stop. We may learn a lesson about a relationship or a financial issue, or it may take yet another trip around the block to get the message. My friend Sylvie says that we will make the same mistake just one more time to make sure that we get the message. Or, as the Buddhist teacher Pema Chödrön advises, we will fall flat on our faces time and again. Such a situation suggests that we need to understand our own journey from a perspective of modest expectations and humility in terms of the limits of our capabilities. I can picture Clint Eastwood as Dirty Harry warning the bad guy, "A man's got to know his limitations!"

These modest expectations extend to our journey with others as well. Human relationships are full of failed expectations. Borrowing from Robert Wild, betrayals, misunderstandings, disappointments, and lack of sensitivities are part of the nature of things. They are built-in limitations because *we are limited*. Perhaps we should say to one another, "Don't be surprised when I don't measure up to all your needs and expectations." Opacity gives rise to the need for much forgiveness and compassion—of self and others—on the journey.

Human wisdom and stillness emerge through hardships and inconsistencies. Things seldom play out according to our expectations. You need the capacity to surrender to events that do not make sense, that make you bewildered and frustrated. The journey to life is an unlikely combination of being able to age, suffer, enjoy, endure, and grow—all at the same time.

The spiritual teacher Sogyal Rinpoche describes the human journey well when he says that we live in a constant state of suspense and ambiguity. We are always shifting in and out of confusion and clarity. Ironically, if we were confused all the time, that would at least make for some kind of clarity. However, what makes you really wonder about life is that sometimes, despite all the confusion, you and I can also be really wise.

I believe we will always have thoughts that reflect the opacity of the journey. These include the following: "I'm still a bit confused about that," "That didn't turn out the way I thought it would," "I really don't quite understand this," "I still have some questions about how I did that," or "What happened there?"

The third guideline is that the indefiniteness of the journey suggests that there may be, at least for practical purposes, no final destination of the journey to life. The real purpose of human life and aging may be the journey itself, or, more precisely, the quality of the journey, and not the destination. It is possible that there are no better or worse paths in life; the real significance is in what you can do with the path of your personal journey and, again, if you can keep your life going as a journey. The best that you can hope for and aspire to is that your voyage will be informed by moments of still-ness, wonder, openness, peace, and even enthusiasm, even though you experience loss, suffering, betrayal, disillusionment, and various forms of *death* on the way. Perhaps the point of the journey is that you are to find life *through* death, as is poignantly represented, for example, in the life of Jesus.

It is the gift of stillness, which arises when you let go, that makes the journey worthwhile. We need to remind ourselves again and again that stillness and wisdom are not reserved for saints and swamis.

Explore your Pathway

Given the conditions of the human journey, can you think of experiences in your life, past or present, where a healthy measure of compassion for yourself or for a fellow traveller would be appropriate?

CHAPTER 16
Nothing to Do, Nowhere to Go
—You Are Okay

AN odd feature of being human is that we live both in clock time and in the timeless present. This means that while there are all kinds of changes constantly occurring inside and outside of us, those changes contain a place of rest. As they say in Tai Chi, there is both movement and stillness. I believe this is something, or more precisely *no-thing*, that is possible to experience, but where language must be seen as only a signpost. However, the point is that perhaps it is true that we should not "sweat the small stuff," and that "it is all small stuff." If we can relax into stillness, then we may be able to find a quiet place within *all* the forms and dramas that swirl within and without.

These forms include relationships, jobs, health, finances, and even thoughts and emotions. This, of course, is easier said than done. But it is possible on the journey to life. If we can embrace even a little of this experience, it can help us to find the third way, beyond fight or flight. This remains a major challenge in my life, as I am a runner. I like to escape from the problem. Nevertheless, I have had some success with this third way in my marriage. When there is a disagreement, I try not to act out in anger (fight) or leave (flight). I try to step back, breathe, and watch myself in the drama. I cannot say that it works all the time (and my wife would agree), but it has made a difference in our relationship. If you can just leave the thinking mind out of the picture for a while—"How dare she say that to me?" "That is her fault," and so on—there is room for a new and better story to emerge together. Nothing to do, nowhere to go means that, at some level, we are all right, even when in the midst of the chaos. A student once pointed out to me that a sign of progress in this part of the journey is that we move from being unaware of our reactions (running, etc.) to at least being aware of them, but for a time, we watch ourselves doing the same old things anyway.

Health is another area of life where this insight can be useful. When we get sick, the thinking mind races back and forth from the past to the future with apocalyptic scenarios: "Is it this?" "I had something like this before." "My friend had this and she—." This is a time when doing our best to relax into stillness, and not generate stories with the thinking mind, can be beneficial to physical and mental health. Granted, this is not like turning on a light switch; that is why many teachers suggest that beginning to practise stillness is always a good thing, so that it will be there when *stuff happens*. So, this short chapter is another reminder that, first, part of you resides in stillness, and, second, you have to show up to connect with it. You do not have to figure out anything, you just need to show up. A wonderful poster I saw in a Buddhist meditation centre in The

Netherlands says, Everything is all right in the end. If it is not all right, it is not the end.

Explore your Pathway

The next time you find yourself in a stressful situation, stop, try a "relax into stillness" movement (found at the end of the book), and then attempt to deal with the story that is unfolding.

CHAPTER 17
Nothing to Do, Nowhere to Go—More Lives?

WHEN you manage to find stillness, you may come to feel that there is really *no time* but the present moment, and that moment feels larger than this lifetime. Everything is just there. This is the paradox of having things to do, but already being there. For example, on a good day I can accept that I will die, but on other days this thought makes me anxious. There may be things about who you are and what you need to do on your journey that you feel may not be completed in the few years that are granted to human beings.

In my case, there are still many interpersonal encounters where I behave in a defensive or selfish way. Progress seems to be very slow in this part of my journey, but I do notice that over time there is some change in the right direction. I try to practise what I preach, which is to be a good friend to myself, forgiving time and again. I try not to beat myself up, and treat myself according to the saying, "A friend is someone who knows everything about you, and still hangs around with you."

In any case, relaxing into stillness offers the possibility that there is no hurry. You are not here to become a perfect human being—you are here to find stillness. This may not be the first time that you are here, nor the last. I believe that this is true. I remember speaking with Brother Leo, my Trappist monk friend, about this issue. The official doctrine of the Catholic Church is that there is no rebirth. However, as we discussed this issue, he said, "Well, If God can put me here once, why could he not put me here again?"

The underlying agenda from this point of view is that you are here to learn. Human nature seems to be a curious combination of frailty and strength of spirit, confusion and clarity, ignorance and wisdom. Paraphrasing the Tibetan Buddhist teacher Sogyal Rinpoche, if you were always confused, that would at least give you some sort of clarity. So your journey appears to be to show up, to try—but not to try too hard, because you need access to stillness, and if you work too hard you will lose that part of yourself. As Brother Leo says, "All you can do is desire to be a saint. God does the rest." The rest that God does may happen now, or it may continue to happen later.

When Buddhists speak about the bigger picture of rebirth, they often refer to the notion of *karma*. They urge you to relax into stillness and be the witness to who you are as a person right now. As a friend to yourself, you may notice habits, tendencies, attitudes, desires, and particular forms of attachments, whether they be to people, objects, feelings (such as loves and fears), or beliefs. They also suggest that who you are now is in part due to who you were in a past life; you arrived in this life as a collection of particular characteristics. For Buddhists, human beings are the only beings

who can be aware of themselves sufficiently, who can practise stillness, with the objective of being free of the attachments that cause
suffering, fear, and so on. By paying attention to your journey, you
may find yourself in a future life with less suffering, more stillness,
more peace. If nothing else, you may find this to be a hopeful and
optimistic view of human life.

Explore your Pathway

After first relaxing into stillness, you may wish to take a look at your
loves and fears, or attachments. You could also include here your
comfort behaviors, which were discussed at the beginning of the
book. But do this in a gentle and compassionate way, being a good
friend to yourself. Also, keep in mind that there is no hurry, since we
are all exactly where we need to be at this moment.

CHAPTER 18
Human, All Too Human

THE journey to life is neither easy nor simple. But in one way it is very simple: all you have to do is relax into stillness. However, as Manuel on *Fawlty Towers* says, "Is easy for you!" When life presents you with suffering or loss, our initial response is often one of denial and closing off, along with a feeling of separation and alienation. You can feel disconnected from your self, your body, other people, and even God. In addition, the movement from separation to acceptance and stillness is not a matter of control and willpower—and that is precisely the problem: you feel out of control and lost. There is no quick fix.

The process of letting go involves a kind of death or emptiness, a feeling of helplessness, frustration, and confusion. Yet if you can somehow allow the situation to be there, very often help comes. Depending on your beliefs, it may be grace, karma, chance, a loving environment, or a combination of the above, but it does come, sometimes in very surprising and unexpected ways. It is almost as though life itself brings you to the point of acceptance and openness to new meaning. As the saying goes, the universe is conspiring in your favour.

Without minimizing the hell you may go through in the initial stages of loss, in the end it is often not a bad thing. Loss and suffering can bring you to stillness, new meaning, wisdom, and the awareness of a larger journey *to* life. Somehow, if you give it a chance, you come to accept life as it is, and not how you want it to be. In this way you find your place in that larger journey, and you may stop *pushing the river*.

Explore your Pathway

When you find your self in a situation of stress or fear try a "relax into stillness" movement and wait a little, rather than giving-up or demanding an immediate resolution to the problem. At first, it may be easier to accomplish this third way in a small life experience, but with practice you can become better at inviting the support from stillness into major life events.

CHAPTER 19
What's the Point?

HUMAN life, as existentialist writers emphasize, can be described as being absurd. You are born, as far as you know, without having chosen where you will be, or, at the very least, not remembering, which amounts to the same thing. As the philosopher Martin Heidegger has said, you are thrown into the world. Things happen to you, many of which you do not choose, and many of which involve loss, separation, pain, and myriad other forms of disillusionment and suffering. On top of this, you know you will die, but not how or when.

If this were not enough, you must also experience the process of aging. To speak about aging as anything resembling a journey to life is, from the outside point of view, patently absurd. From a biological point of view, you mature and develop early in life, and then begin to decline. If you do not die, you have eventual frailty to which to look forward. As biologists say, the longer you live, the less chance you have of survival. As one older person said to me, "There are many discounts you are eligible for, but after that there is nothing much to be said for it." This would appear to be the description of a quintessential absurd situation—even an invitation to despair.

To add insult to injury, virtually all spiritual traditions and thinkers invite us to surrender to this situation. We are told that, somehow, suffering, which takes away, can awaken us to a larger journey toward meaning and peace. We are told that resisting this process is like being on a journey with our brakes on. Other writers on this topic, such as Sogyal Rinpoche, tell us that pain, loss, and ceaseless frustration are there to wake us up, to release our imprisoned splendour. In other words, we are told that not only are we suffering, but that it's our problem that we do not get the point of it all.

Those who argue that the human condition is absurd do have a point. Who in their right mind would choose to welcome an illness, suffer chronic pain, be separated from loved ones, endure loneliness, be slowly lost to dementia, or watch their child kill herself through drug addiction? But is this the end of the story of the human predicament? Perhaps these spiritual writers are correct, and we need to look at our journey in a different way. Or are they all fooling themselves, denying the awful reality of life?

The key to this story having a different ending—or at least an ongoing life-affirming plot—has to do with looking more closely at our own aging and changing, but from the inside. That is where stillness and our ordinary wisdom reside, both of which can bring less suffering and more peace to our lives.

Explore your Pathway

It is healthy to acknowledge the absurd aspects of human life. However, if you are willing to relax into stillness and calm your monkey mind, you may discover that absurdity is not "the only story in town". You may discover that even though it makes no sense, the harder and illogical aspects of life actually provide you with your pathway to stillness.

PART B:
Tai Chi Wisdom

The stories in this section are about pathways inspired and flavoured by my experiences with the art of Tai Chi.

CHAPTER 20
Self-Defence

DID you know that the majority of illnesses we experience these days are, in one way or another, stress- and lifestyle-related? In addition, there is a shortage of medical doctors, so it is more difficult to find one when you need one. Then there is the problem of side effects from many medications that we may have to take to relieve pain or otherwise deal with a particular health condition. Given all this, I consider stillness practice a form of self-defence, since stillness works. There is substantial research now that demonstrates the beneficial aspects of stillness practice. Stillness can help you live a longer and healthier life.

Stillness resides in the present moment, where there is no time. This space gives you the opportunity to have some fun while learning on your journey, as you are not distracted by past performance or future objectives. This is the serious play mantra of Tai Chi. The *serious* part requires you to focus, to pay attention, and the *play* part allows your creative side to emerge: it allows for new stories, new meaning—in other words, it creates conditions for the emergence of your ordinary wisdom. Tai Chi as an art form is your personal canvas for mind, body, and spirit as you move through the changes on your journey to life.

(By the way, serious play is not unique to Tai Chi, which is my main art form. It is present in perhaps all creative endeavours. Whether it is music, visual arts, writing, or even athletics, the process is similar. There is a form or structure; learning scales in music, colour theory in drawing, learning to skate and stickhandle in hockey, the 108 traditional Tai Chi form, or a variation of these.)

While you may not have access to a Tai Chi class, I would like to talk about why this art is a very effective pathway to stillness. You may be able to apply this wisdom to a pathway that is accessible to you. I will begin by offering an overview of what Tai Chi is:

Tai Chi is based on Taoist philosophy. Much of this philosophy can be understood by looking at the two concepts of yin and yang. The symbol of this philosophy—a circle containing black and white areas with a curved line through the middle—is very familiar these days, as it is a logo for all sorts of products and services—sneakers, health food products, cereal boxes, and a variety of clinics. Yin and yang refer to types of energy, and are divided into such pairs as female-male, dark-light, moon-sun, and receptive-aggressive. The universe and all things in it, including us human beings, function on the basis of combinations of these energies. Taoist philosophy claims that a balance of yin and yang energies in the world, and in you, promotes stillness, health, and peace. Imbalance causes the opposite: illness, war, and suffering in general.

Tai Chi, being based on this philosophy, is specifically designed to help you find health and peace. It does this through a particular set of physical movements and ways of breathing. But more than this, it encourages you to develop an attitude of slowing down and paying attention to the present moment, thus allowing stillness to enter your life.

The hallmark of Tai Chi is yin, or female energy, and that is why it can be so helpful in the world today. At this time in history there is too much yang energy, and that is why we are destroying our environment. It is also the cause of the epidemic of stress-related illness. For many, life is all stress and no stillness. Tai Chi, as strange as it may sound at first, talks about such things as investing in loss, letting go, becoming soft and empty, allowing, following, and yielding. The most difficult part of Tai Chi as a martial art is learning to let go, to stop resisting, and to give up immediate control, something you otherwise automatically do, either through fight or flight. It really is a *third way* beyond these two ways of reacting to stressful situations. This is not easy to achieve because these two options are almost part of our hardwiring as human beings.

Nevertheless, it is possible and, once learned, even to a small degree, your life can take on a different flavour and direction. Also, you do not need to study Tai Chi as a martial art to get there: rather, it is a way of being in the world, an attitude. (You can begin to work toward this way of being by performing the "relax into stillness movements" recommended at the end of this book, and by trying to apply the themes in the stillness stories. It is not about giving up; it is about giving in when the big winds blow in your life.)

In Tai Chi, the first level is to learn a choreographed set of movements that originated a very long time ago. The second step is to begin learning the concept or purpose of each movement. This can be done for health or meditation purposes, or, if you are interested, for martial art applications. The third step is to learn to make the form seamless, like one movement. This is called *stillness in movement*, as the purpose is to experience stillness while performing the form. You also gradually learn to use your chi (your "vital energy") and to breathe deeply. All this is done to enhance your stillness experience.

In reality, as you continue to learn, you will go back and forth among the levels of practice, including a regular return to the beginning, which is called form refinement. You never get to the end. The work is to be patient, focused, and determined to learn the basics of the art, yet it should also be fun, as you have chosen to learn the art. But as you progress, the emphasis is less on the basic techniques and more on playing inside the form.

This is where the stillness lies, whether it is your own life or any other artistic pursuit. The form is always new, always changing with practice and with inner and outer circumstances. You may notice this when you say that someone is *in the zone*, which means that they seem to be at one with what they are doing. Again, you may also sense this with athletes, musicians, actors, writers, and painters. They are expressing stillness. And you may also notice this phenomenon with experienced plumbers, carpenters, and electricians. When they encounter a problem, they just seem to *know* or figure out how to do something that is far beyond their technical training, and, in the process, they learn something new. Even your work can be a stillness practice.

Explore your Pathway

If you feel so inclined, relax into stillness to calm your monkey mind. Then you might wish to begin to consider how you can move toward seeing your life as serious play. Give yourself permission to step back from your obligations and allow stillness to be part of your decision-making in your personal life, relationships, and work life. This may be challenging at first, but as the Taoists saying goes, the journey of ten thousand miles begins with the first step.

CHAPTER 21
The Right Way to Practice?

WHEN you begin stillness practice, whatever form it may take—Tai Chi, yoga, meditation, or something else—you may wonder what is the right way to practice. You may also find many answers to this question, from teachers, books, and other practitioners. Here are my guidelines:

Time. Is there a recommended time of day? In most spiritual traditions, practice is held at dawn. The idea is that at this time your thinking mind is more at rest and you are more receptive to stillness on the inside. There are also fewer distractions, so stillness is more accessible on the outside as well. I think there is some merit in this view; however, it is not a necessity. If it works for you to do this practice, go for it. However, if it does not work, do not beat yourself up or decide not to bother with the practice. I do rise at 3:30 a.m. when I visit my favourite monastery. Otherwise, I seldom get up that early for anything. You can fit your time of practice to your lifestyle and to your schedule. A regular time every day is helpful, especially at first. Later on, you may be able to practice whenever the opportunity presents itself in the day, whenever you can *steal* some time just for you. That is how I often practice now, after many years of stillness practice.

Length of session. How long to practice? There is no set duration. If you meditate, at first you may feel that you are going crazy. So you may not last longer than a few minutes. In reality, what is happening is that you are, perhaps for the first time, paying attention to your mind, and thus experiencing your *monkey mind* full out. If you give it a chance and try to practice a few more times, you will probably discover that you feel good for a longer period, perhaps five minutes, then ten, and so on, as you are comfortable. In Tai Chi practice, some teachers advise a minimum of one hour or more per day, making sure that you practice your form and other exercises. Again, I would say to do what you can, when you can. Of course, you will benefit more the more you place yourself in stillness, but only if you enjoy it. Chinese philosophy calls Tai Chi *serious play*, not work or obligation. How can you relax if you feel it is a burden to practice? Also, it is more beneficial to practice for a shorter time more often than one day a week for a longer period. There is one other open secret here: the more you practice, the more you will want to do so—the stillness will draw you in and help you practice.

No thoughts. Should your mind be empty of thoughts? This may be possible for some, but I have not met anyone who can do this for more than a few seconds. The objective is not to be empty of thoughts but to become a better witness, to watch your monkey mind without being drawn into its endless chatter. You will also find that you become more aware when you are, on the one hand, present, mindful, or still, and, on the other hand, lost or distracted.

The more you catch yourself being distracted and gently return to the stillness, the more peaceful you become.

Position. Is there a recommended practice posture? There are traditional positions such as the full-lotus posture in yoga and positions in Tai Chi and Chi Kung. I have never been able to accomplish cross-legged immobility, as one of my friends calls it. Thankfully, more and more teachers are encouraging students to first be comfortable, sit on a chair, or do whatever is needed to do to relax. Do what you can handle, which means you will be more willing and interested to try out the practice. Tai Chi, for example, is adaptable to just about any level of fitness or frailty. In the hands of a good teacher, the movements can be performed to your individual limits. You can find more discussion about this in other stillness stories in this book, but to summarize: the practice can be done standing or sitting; each movement can be adjusted to accommodate specific physical and even mental challenges, as with dementia survivors.

On the other hand, for interested practitioners, Tai Chi practice can become very complex, detailed, and subtle. The most important thing to remember is that the practice needs to help you to relax and thus bring you to stillness. In the end, it is not about what you are doing but about how you are feeling. This reminds me of a meditation class I experienced a few years ago. The teacher asked the class what was the guaranteed best way to tell that your meditation session was successful. Some participants said that they became quiet, others that they saw light. This went on for a while, and then the teacher said, "Anything else?" My wife, Liz, spoke up and said, "That it is over." The teacher remarked, "There is a wise person!"

CHAPTER 22
Just Practice

WHETHER it is life itself—often in the form of suffering and loss—or a formal or informal meditation practice, the goal is to bring you beyond the thinking mind. However, as we also saw in Chapter 21, meditation is not about never having thoughts, or having visions, or remaining in a state of cross-legged bliss. In my view, meditation works when you can be in a state of acceptance and openness, with no expectations. Meditation is about showing up and seeing what happens.

I agree with Thomas Merton, the writer and Trappist monk, who suggests that you should not judge the value of your meditation by how you feel. A hard and apparently wasted meditation session may in fact be much more valuable than one that is easy, happy, and enlightened—one that you think is a big success. When I first read Merton's insights, I felt great relief and space in my meditation practice. When I sit now, I try to feel that it is not that I need to be doing something, but rather that stillness is working on me, and that I am being guided. It is not important how I feel or what is happening in my practice session. I just show up!

My other favourite Trappist, Brother Leo, who is now eighty-nine and has been a monk for more than sixty years, tells the following story. He said that when he gets to heaven, if God says to him, "Why are you not a saint?" he will say to God, "Well, I asked you many, many times, so it is your fault that I am not a saint." He believes that God will agree with him that it is God's fault. The point is to just show up and practice and let go of any goal. There really is nothing next.

However, you do need to show up regularly. Once more I defer to Brother Leo, who says, "If I don't pray regularly, things don't feel as good; I lose some of my peace." I am like Brother Leo. The main reason I practice is that I feel better when I do. When I invite stillness into my day, I feel better in my skin, and the day just seems to go more peacefully. This is aside from the fact that sometimes I feel complete peace: I feel loved and safe—that all is right with the world. It is easy to practice on those days.

Another liberating insight about meditation comes from Eckhart Tolle. He suggests that as meditation practice continues, it is not how long you can stay in a thoughtless state, but how often you become aware that you are thinking. A thousand thoughts means a thousand opportunities to return to the question. In my experience, I find myself becoming aware of thinking more and more often, which means I remain longer in stillness.

My own stillness practice is an example of *applied ecumenism*. Over the years, it has included a basic Buddhist meditation—following the breath period—a short prayer that is chanted in a Trappist monastery, a series of *pranayama* breathing exercises that I learned from a friend who teaches yoga, and a prayer list of those I feel are particularly in need that day, including myself. Later in the day I include my Tai Chi practice. I mention this routine to highlight the fact that there is not necessarily a confusion or contradiction in integrating practices from different traditions in your personal journey. I would, however, qualify this statement by saying that it is important that you do not simply shop around the *spiritual supermarket* and, therefore, not deepen your practice itself. To do so would simply be another way of going *around* your journey instead of *through* it.

It is helpful to have a main path that makes the most sense to you and which will take you deeper into your practice. Thomas Merton remained a Catholic priest and Trappist monk, but he had a deep appreciation of Buddhism and Taoism, which were a part of his spiritual life. My own stillness practice these days is a combination of Tai Chi and its philosophy of Taoism, along with Buddhist meditation.

It is also helpful, and perhaps necessary at certain times, to have a teacher or spiritual friend. As Thomas Merton points out, even contemplatives who devote their lives to prayer can fall into the trap of simply repeating words or practicing in such a way that promotes *playing* a religious role. In this way, the practice loses its aliveness— its effectiveness in cultivating the spirit and furthering your journey. In my experience, this is a common occurrence among those who do not have a context for continued learning, whatever path they choose. Your monkey mind is very clever and can subtly create a story about stillness that masks the real experience.

However, these stories are not the reality. This is what is meant when the Buddha said, "I must state clearly that my teaching is a method to experience reality and not reality itself, just as a finger pointing at the moon is not the moon itself." And, as Lao Tzu wrote in the *Tao Te Ching*, "The Tao that can be spoken is not the eternal Tao." The lesson here is if you think you are making progress, forget it. Things happen when you are out of your mind! You cannot be in stillness and in your mind at the same time.

Stillness practice can become a trap in yet another way. It can produce a false sense of serenity, security, and even smugness. Stillness as a way of life can help you connect to the world and fellow beings in a kinder and more flexible way, but it can also provide a subtle tool for avoiding and denying issues, internal and external. Strange, but you can become self-absorbed with the feeling of peace and lose your sensitivity to and compassion for others. That is why it is very useful on your journey to use relax-into-stillness practice, as well as stillness stories and by exploring your pathway. In this way you continue to learn from the larger story that you live within.

There is a basic paradox in the wisdom of stillness. On the one hand, you need to have a desire for stillness; you need to show up to life and your practice. On the other hand, you are asked to accept, trust, and surrender to whatever comes, and to follow. You need to be active in showing up and then receptive to what happens after that. You are asked to make an effort without expecting any progress, reward, or feelings of achievement. An expectation of progress is counterproductive because it presumes an understanding of exactly where you are going, the efforts of your intellect and imagination notwithstanding

Without contradicting what I just said about expectations, you can observe progress on your journey to life over time, but you have to approach it carefully—kind of out of the corner of your eye—and you cannot take it for granted. With practice, you do feel more stillness in your life, and you can bring more stillness to everyday experiences. However, paraphrasing the Dalai Lama, spiritual progress takes time. It's not like switching on a light. It is more like kindling a fire as it starts from a small spark, and then becomes bigger. He also says that progress is not noticeable at first; results are often seen clearly only after many years. Nevertheless, you are on a journey to stillness and to more life.

CHAPTER 23
A Larger View

IF allowing, yielding, losing, becoming soft, do not mean giving up or resigning yourself to a situation, what do they mean? The idea is that when an overwhelming force comes at you, whether it is emotional or physical, rather than collapsing in despair or stubbornly attempting to fix or control the situation, you first *step back*. As one of my students said, you step back to get a larger view. In Tai Chi this is called neutralizing the force, bringing it to nothing. As in *Star Trek*, there is a non-interference directive. You are then better able to respond to the force in a way that goes toward restoring your balance, health, and stillness. By operating with stillness as part of the equation, you have a better chance to learn something worthwhile from stressful experiences, and to thereby enhance your journey to life.

Don't push the river
Tai Chi philosophy tells us that human life itself is yang energy, meaning that it is a stressor. Tai Chi is yin energy because it attempts to balance that stressor by receiving, accepting, and neutralizing. Tai

Chi involves a giving in, but by no means does it involve a giving up. It is not resignation but acceptance, which means that you attempt to follow the situation until it can be brought to a balanced or healthy conclusion. You are asked to blend with the oncoming force, meet it, follow it and, eventually, direct it. You try to not interfere with the momentum of the force, whether physical or emotional. In other words, do not push the river.

There is a parallel to these principles in the profession of marine engineering. A good friend of mine, Stig, asked me what I was writing about, and when I described this book, he said that was exactly what he does in his work. When he designs a small dock to accommodate a 200,000-tonne ship, he needs to do more than just build a dock. With nothing else there, the ship would destroy any dock upon minimal impact. Therefore, Stig designs a system of fenders that will yield to and absorb the force generated by the ship. Tai Chi philosophy talks about the strength of four ounces being able to deal with the force of one thousand pounds. Upon reflection, this makes sense, since both approaches deal with natural forces. In either case, confronting a force head on is not a wise way to proceed.

In my experience, arriving at the point of yielding takes a great deal of showing up to practice, regularly *losing* to a partner who has already learned to let go and be empty, and who is therefore able to follow whatever you are giving them. In Tai Chi there is a saying that is reminiscent of Jesus: If you try to save yourself, you will lose. However, this is precisely why Tai Chi can be an effective pathway to surrender, wisdom, and stillness in your life. Little by little, we learn to let go of our physical and emotional resistance and trust that we are okay. It is a way for us to see that giving in does not mean giving up, and that there is strength in diminishment and loss.

Over time, I have gradually been able to apply this to situations of stress and crisis. Still, there can always be situations that take us completely by surprise, and then the practice goes out the window temporarily. Repeating a basic theme of this book, the journey as an *existential ride* always remains all too human. At these times you may follow the advice of Eckhart Tolle: If you cannot surrender, then surrender to the fact that you cannot surrender. This is better than simply resisting or totally giving up, which are choices that create the most suffering in your life and rob you of your stillness.

Explore your Pathway

The next time you encounter a stressful situation try first to step back instead of running or resisting. A stillness practice of your choice will be of great help in developing this attitude. These could include yoga, mindfulness practice, meditation, and "relax into stillness" movements at the end of this book.

CHAPTER 24
Mr. No

THERE are other forms of surrender or yielding in Tai Chi. As I have previously stated, Tai Chi is an art form. As such, the ego needs to give in to the fact that there is no end point to reach, no ultimate success where you can say that you have *made it.* There is only continuous refinement of the moves and the principles of the art. At some point, doing the form in Tai Chi is done for its own sake, because it is there. There is always something to learn, both from the form and from other practitioners. Your practice is creative and alive, fresh with each performance of the form. Even after many years of practice—in my case about thirty years of martial art teaching and learning, more than half of that Tai Chi—there are days when I feel that I have only begun to learn what this art is about, and I am in awe of its profundity. On other days, it all seems to come together, and there is a feeling of tremendous stillness and connectedness with what is around me.

Even though you need to drop all expectations of progress, over time you will feel that the baseline of your practice is getting stronger; the stillness gets deeper. That is the difference between this kind of practice and many other things in life. In traditional Tai Chi, there are no belts or other external recognitions of progress or achievement. You simply practice for yourself and deepen your art little by little.

Pathways to stillness are challenging if you are accustomed to a payoff, a reward for achievement, and an ultimate goal at which to arrive. In my own development as a practitioner, I was fortunate to have a karate *sensei* (teacher) who, contrary to common practice in karate, held back our belts, especially the black belt. His hope was that by the time we received our black belts, we would be training only for our personal growth. This experience helped me move beyond the achievement and competitive tyranny I grew up with, where there was always competition, winners and losers, instead of mutual sharing and camaraderie.

In my present Tai Chi practice, I call our head instructor (Si Kung), who visits us about once a year, Mr. No. This is because he lines us up in the training hall and tells us to show him a particular part of the form. Then he points to each of us and says, "No-no-no-no." We look forward to this admonition, as it is his way to encourage us to let go of what we have learned up to that point, so he can teach us something new. The new refinement builds on what we have practised before, but if we hang on to the old information, we cannot learn the new stuff. We need to be willing to continually go back to the beginning. As with other pathways to stillness, in Tai Chi we simply need to show up and surrender to the journey that is larger than us as individuals—a journey that has its own ways that our thinking mind cannot fathom. The journey to life is not a do-it-yourself project.

CHAPTER 25
Unexpected Stillness

STILLNESS, and its inherent peacefulness, is accessible anytime and anywhere. I agree with those who say it is our natural state, covered over by the monkey mind and distractions. A very powerful example of this is a particular Tai Chi class that I teach at York Care Centre in Fredericton, New Brunswick, the city where I work. I have been teaching classes in various locations for over twenty years, and in nursing homes and retirement residences for ten years. Some years ago, I was invited by the activity director of the centre to try a class in the Alzheimer unit. I agreed, without any expectations. I arrived for the class, and put a CD on with soft music.

The staff person asked the residents if they would like to attend and assisted them to gather in the lounge area. Six residents sat down and watched me as I began the class, which, by the way, is a seated program, which I designed for special groups. One resident was able to follow many of the movements; two had their eyes closed and were clearly listening to the music; another was sleeping; and two were staring at me with curiosity. But there was something else happening at the same time: there was a palpable stillness in the room, a wonderful peacefulness. In subsequent classes, I sometimes sense this peacefulness and I stop talking and just hang out with them.

I discussed the results of the class with the staff person. She said what happens here is huge. These are folks who are constantly in motion, who do not usually sit still for more than a few minutes, who often have fear and confusion in their eyes. However, during this class they are quiet and their eyes are calm—the staff person agreed that they clearly felt the stillness. To me this means that, unlike the stereotype that dementing persons are totally lost, there is also a still-ness present—they are *still* there.

I continue to learn many lessons from this group: First, we should not make quick assumptions about what is going on within a person with dementia. Just because a person's thinking mind is confused does not mean that they cannot experience stillness. One of my Dutch colleagues conducts a similar class in The Netherlands. She says that when they are doing Tai Chi, "the disease is not there and we go straight to the stillness." Second, these folks are able to contribute to *my* experience of stillness when I am sharing the class with them. And third, as I mentioned at the outset, stillness is possible anywhere and anytime. If they can find it, so can you.

As I mentioned, I have been teaching a *seated* Tai Chi class for ten years at several retirement residences. In all my classes, I attempt to create an atmosphere of non-judgmental acceptance and silence, conditions that allow stillness to emerge. One class is composed mostly of residents who are physically challenged, but they do very well following the movements.

There are several staff members, chronologically younger than the residents, who attend every class. This particular participant, Joyce* (not her real name), has *special abilities* and usually shadows another staff member in her daily work activities. About four years ago, she began attending the class. Although she attended regularly (accompanied by another staff member), she would not look directly at me, preferring to sit in the back of the class behind all the other participants. She did not perform any movements. After some time I would hear her humming to the soft music I always play in the session. I began saying hello to her when she arrived at the class. No response.

Then one day I said hi—and she said hi back to me. For me this was a big deal; it meant that a connection happened. As more time passed, Joyce began attending on her own and performing many of the movements. Then, about a year ago, a wonderful thing happened. At the end of the class, we always perform a move called Wave Hands Like Clouds. I started to announce this move and Joyce said, "Wave hands like clouds." For her to feel comfortable enough to participate in this way brought tears to my eyes. This has now developed into a ritual where I point to Joyce and she announces the move.

There is one more step in this story. At the end of a number of weekly sessions, at Christmas and Easter, I ask for hugs from everyone. Joyce looks into my eyes and gives me a big hug. Stillness works!

---

*   The name and other details have been changed to respect the anonymity of this participant.

CHAPTER 26
Awakening Stillness

STILLNESS cannot be forced. It plays by its own rules. That is why it cannot be accessed by your thinking mind—any effort of this kind just covers it over. I remember watching a film in which researchers were trying to identify a mystical experience, which is a kind of stillness experience, in the brain. They asked one of the nun participants to tell them when she was having such an experience. She said that it is not possible to have the experience and talk about it at the same time. One experience rules out the other. However, there are conditions that will make it more possible for stillness to make itself known to you. These conditions are to show up, calm down, be present, and to not have any expectations as to what stillness is about.

This is actually very challenging at first. We are accustomed from childhood to achieve, to compete with others, to perform or measure up to some objective, and to feel that we have failed if we do not. Thus, the most difficult part of teaching my Tai Chi classes is to create an environment in which the participants will be open to letting go of this way of thinking. Whether you are fit or frail, older or younger, you still have self-esteem needs and a need for acceptance without judgment.

I encourage this wisdom, or *stillness environment*, in my classes with special groups in nursing homes and retirement settings by regularly reminding participants that you are there only to *relax*. These are my reminders: you can try the movements; you should not do anything that is uncomfortable; you can have a nap; or you can just listen to the music. They begin to experience stillness when they drop the need to measure up to a standard besides their own, and when they trust and accept me as just another member of the class. They have to feel that I am not there to pity them, improve them, or judge their performance.

Once this situation is happening in the class, and they give themselves permission to just *be themselves*, wonderful things are possible. I will suggest that a movement can be done with one arm or one hand, and someone with one arm will try it. Clifford, who cannot move his legs at all and one arm only minimally, moves his fingers. Raymond, who has motor skill issues, will perform a movement totally different from the one I am sharing, but he is moving and always tells me how much he enjoys the class.

These classes work because we all meet in a space of trust, calmness, and being present to each other, prime conditions for the emergence of stillness. It is a precious connection. Paradoxically, I feel that my friends in these special classes feel stillness more quickly · because, at least from an outside point of view, they do not *have* much. Perhaps being present is easier if you have fewer distractions. This does not mean that they have no issues and challenges to face, like you do, but perhaps they can be role models for your search for stillness on your journey to life.

Explore your Pathway

As you meander on your journey seeking new stillness practices, you might wish to keep in mind the guidelines for a stillness environment just described. Whether it is a solitary practice or a group setting, try to cultivate in yourself an attitude of curiosity and relaxation. Give yourself permission to not get something right the first time, or even not at all. But even before that step, give yourself permission to try something new—just go for it. You may wish to use the "relax into stillness" movements as a way to prepare yourself before starting something new. Many of the students in my courses at university find them helpful at exam time.

CHAPTER 27
The Magic is in the Details

HERE are more stories of what is possible in the stillness environment of my Tai Chi classes with special groups. A precious soul-to-soul connection is created that invites stillness into their lives and mine. Think of what is possible in your own life if you can approach others in this accepting, non-judgmental way. As I heard the Dalai Lama once say with an attitude of openness and acceptance, "Oh! Another human being". Much stillness can happen by paying a little more attention and being a little more present to each other. Granted, it is much more challenging in the busy-ness of daily life, but that makes it even more important.

Flo

Flo attended one class. After the class she said she was ninety-three years old and full of arthritis, so she could not do the exercises. I said she was welcome to come and listen to the music and relax with us. She said, "Okay, it will be like an outing with other residents." She returned to the next class and proceeded to do most of the movements.

Dr. Smith

One day I was explaining the health benefits of Tai Chi, the breathing and its benefits on the nervous system, and I acknowledged Dr. Smith, a long-retired medical doctor. I said, "You know much more than me about these things." A very moved expression appeared on his face, and he said, "Thank you very much for that."

Monty

Monty comes every week to class. She does not do any of the movements and sometimes sleeps, but she does look very involved in the music and watching me. One day I asked her if she liked the music. She motioned me over and whispered, "Of all the things they have us do here, this is my favourite." Another day I asked her why her foot was bandaged. She called me over and apologized that she could not do all the exercises as before because she fell off a horse, and asked if she could attend class anyway. I said, "Just be careful with your leg." Two weeks later I asked her if she had been riding lately, She said, "Oh, no, I don't do that anymore."

Origato

This gentleman, Woody, always bows to me with joined hands; he is a Korean veteran. He sometimes says he is tired because this is the second time he has done the exercises today. You never know! After a year or so in the class, Woody now cannot follow most of the exercises; he tells me he is doing his best with what he has. I did get a big smile from him when I reminded him of how we always bow to each other, and we did so.

Clifford

Clifford can only move one hand. He does not speak except to say hi. One day I noticed that he was sitting in the back of the room and looked sad. I said, "Clifford, I think you like to sit in the front, don't you?" He grabbed my hand and held it tight and his eyes brightened. I helped him move to the front.

Jackie

I call Jackie the "queen of the one-liners." She agrees that she has been good at that all her life. One day I said that we were going to begin with some breathing exercises. She said, "Well, I don't know about anyone else here, but I am still breathing."

Another day I was explaining how yawning in a Tai Chi class is a compliment because it means the person is relaxing. She asked, "What about sleeping and snoring?" She said she can sleep any-where. I said, "I guess that would be okay too." Then, after a pause, she said, "Even on the toilet." One day I was explaining that in one of the movements you imagine that your hands are falling off the ends of your arms. "But I need them!" she said. The group erupted in laughter.

Another time she said that she could not bend over to pick up her hands. One day she said that I am always talking about circles in Tai Chi. She said there are no "squares" in Tai Chi, with the intended double meaning. At another session I mentioned something about peace in Tai Chi that might be like something from God. She said that God can count every hair on our heads, but He could not count any on my head (because I have very little).

Isobel

Isobel always sat beside me. I missed her if she did not come to class. One day I asked the others why she was not there. One lady said, "Oh! It is a big day for her. It is her ninety-fifth birthday." Isobel passed away a short time ago in her 102nd year and came to class until one month before she died.

Raymond

Raymond did not talk or do any of the movements for the first four weeks. Then—surprise—he started to do some of the exercises. One day I told him he looked like my father who had died some years ago, especially with his ball cap. I was rewarded with a big smile. Then I asked him his name, Raymond. That was my father's name. We shared an even bigger smile together.

Mother of student

The mother of a former university student of mine attends my class regularly. She never speaks, but she performs all the movements and has a resplendent smile on her face.

Ruth

Ruth attended classes for two years. One day she said that her eyesight had worsened and that she could not see me. I suggested that I could call out the moves and help her position her hands and arms until she was familiar with the moves. She did not return for many months. Then one day she recently returned to class. I again made the offer to assist, and she is now back in class.

Did you miss me?

When we do a short meditation session in the class, I always say at the end, "Open your eyes and return to the room as you may have gone somewhere pleasant for a while." One day a lady said, "Did you miss me?"

Bernice

I went to see a friend who is now in a nursing home. She encouraged me over twenty years ago to start teaching Tai Chi in my community. She was also one of the older adult instructors in a program we designed, which was entitled High Time. She continued to teach her class until about two years ago, the longest-running of the groups. The staff at the nursing home told me that she recognized my name when they mentioned it. She was very happy to see me; however, for most of the visit she thought I was her son. She hugged me and cried and told me that I was a wonderful man, etc. It took me a little while to adjust, but I decided that if this made her feel better, it was fine with me. I am going to bring a couple of tapes of her doing Tai Chi and of her being interviewed. She may appreciate them, but the staff would also like to see her in this role, as a way of getting to know her better.

Cathie

After taking three classes, this student came up to me at the end of the class and said, "I feel very relaxed and I can't think of anything." She added, "I do not remember ever feeling this way before. Is this what is supposed to happen?" In response I said, "You got it!"

Student

A quote from a student: "Tai Chi is a form of meditation and Tai Chi is a form of medication."

Helen

Helen tells me every so often that coming to the Tai Chi class is like a cheap vacation. It is not free, though, because you do have to show up!

Bill

This gentleman said nothing and did not move much during the class. When I asked if there were any questions, he said, "Yeah, how much do they pay you to do this stuff, anyway?"

The code

At the end of one class, I was waiting in the entrance to leave the building. I realized that I needed a code to open the door. A member of the class who had said nothing and not moved at all was sitting in his wheelchair near the door. I called out to ask if someone could let me out. This gentleman eased over to me and in a low voice said, "One, five, two, six."

High five

Therese is a resident in the dementia unit of York Care Centre. One day when I was teaching a Tai Chi class, I noticed her walking the halls. At one point I had my arm in the air performing the move called "Heaven and Earth." Therese came over, stood right in front of me, and high-fived the raised arm. She then continued roaming the halls. About ten minutes later, she returned and stood in front of me again. I raised the arm and invited her to high-five me again. She smiled, did so, and off she went again. This has now become a weekly routine—at least three times in every half-hour class. The staff person thinks this is remarkable because Therese clearly recognizes me and knows what to expect. For me, it is an example of the disease temporarily disappearing in the stillness.

Explore your Pathway

I invite you to think of ways in which you could be more present to others in your professional or personal life. In my work as a gerontologist we call this "practicing narrative care". It means that we try to slow down a little and listen to another person's story, either their words or actions. It is a simple approach but it does take some stillness practice. It can be as easy as taking a moment to acknowledge the cashier in the grocery store by being present to them as a unique person. This practice can stop time and bring a wonderful moment of stillness to both of you. Perhaps this moment could reduce stress and change the tone of your day!

PART C:
Special Persons, Special Events

The stillness stories in this section are about pathways
inspired by special persons and special events in my life.

CHAPTER 28
My Refuges

A refuge is a place or a space where you can avail yourself of an extra boost to reach stillness or an extra boost of stillness. A refuge provides a break from your own stuff: anxieties, confusion, fears, loneliness, monkey mind. It also gives you a break from the stuff you feel loved ones are feeling—that is, their suffering. My daughter Christina says it is "taking a break from your head." Refuges restore balance and peace, and give you inspiration to keep going on the journey. My own refuges include reading particular books written by those I consider wise and helpful, along with spending time with good friends, and cultivating my solitary practice. My lessons from other stillness practitioners appear in many chapters in this book, as do my insights about solitary practice, the latter especially in Chapter 37, "A Sunlit Absence."

There are other refuges (I need many of them) that are particularly meaningful to me. These include a Trappist monastery, Wu's Tai Chi Academy, The Cedar Tree Café, and Breakfast at the Point. In all the settings involving other travellers, the group environment is supportive by being accepting and non-judgmental—what Bill

Randall and I call a *wisdom environment*. These refuges can help you feel comfortable and safe enough to just let go of the baggage. The result is that everyone in the class or group shares the stillness that you create together in the room. The settings differ; what works as a stillness refuge for me may be totally inappropriate for you. Much depends on your interests and temperament. My wife, Liz, once came to pick me up at the Trappist monastery and could not last there for more than an hour—it felt too claustrophobic for her. Yet she can go out in nature or sit on the beach near our home and feel stillness there. There is no recipe for stillness. Stillness is personal, but universally available.

The Trappist monastery

The monastery has been an important refuge for me for twenty-five years. When I arrive there, I place my car keys and wallet in the desk drawer and leave it all behind until I depart. One monk, Brother Leo (whom I mention a number of times in this book) is in charge of the guest house. He is eighty-nine years old at the time of writing and still works and prays all day. He is usually the only monk I talk to when on retreat, unless I have special permission.

The monks, whom you also meet in Chapter 29, pray seven times a day, between 3:30 a.m. and 7:30 p.m. The balance of the day is open for working, reading, walking, sleeping, or just doing nothing. My favourite *offices* (the term for the prayer times) are the 3:30 a.m. and the final one at 7:30 p.m. By the way, I do not get up at 3:30 to do anything when I am at home, except maybe to visit the washroom. But there is something magical and inspiring to listen to the chanting of these seekers just before sunrise. Also, there is a period of silent meditation at the end of the office, and I get a big boost of stillness by sitting in complete silence with nine others. I can understand why contemplatives live in community, even though they are each on their own unique journey to life.

When I am not in the chapel with the monks, my day is composed of quiet and leisurely meals (the food is very good), taking a nap, walking the grounds, reading, practising Tai Chi, and sometimes writing. If there are others there on retreat, there is conversation in the dining room; however, I try to keep this to a minimum. I have to admit that the odd time I will get bored. Boredom, like loneliness (as described in Chapter 12), can be a good thing. It can initiate the act of letting go, which in turn allows stillness to emerge. I do use this as a practice, but at other times I take off to the nearby town for an ice cream. I always bring one back for Brother Leo as well, a treat he really enjoys!

Wu's Tai Chi academy

The academy is a very different stillness setting. The classes are set up to short-circuit the monkey mind right from the beginning. You are instructed to just relax and try to learn and give it your own best effort. As mentioned earlier, Tai Chi is often called *serious play*. In class we will try to *get* a movement that we are practicing with the teacher. Sometimes it happens, sometimes not. At some point before we become frustrated and negative, we say, "Okay, that's it. Time for tea."

There is little intellectual discussion of Taoist philosophy or the science of human movement. The head teacher of the Wu style (Si Kung), whom you met in Chapter 24, visits our club periodically from Hong Kong. When someone is beginning to use their thinking mind too much, he will ask, "Do you only *understand* it or do you *have* it?" Or, when a question is asked, he will say, "Show me." The point of this approach is to put the monkey mind in the background in order to benefit from the stillness of the movement. This does not mean that there is never any discussion of how the moves work. However, this direct approach avoids the easy temptation to mistake the finger for the moon. Tai Chi brings you little by little to your own natural stillness. Too much thinking gets in the way of this natural experience.

The group setting in Tai Chi classes does not promote competition, but rather mutual respect for both your strengths and weaknesses. It is the quality of effort that counts. There is often a special stillness experience when anywhere from four to a dozen of us are performing the Tai Chi *form*, a set of choreographed movements, usually led by Sifu Martin, and which you often see performed in parks around the world. This is done in unison, with soft music or in silence. You need to gently focus on each move, or the rhythm will be disrupted for you and everyone else. Thus everyone is, to their own degree, in stillness. There can be a feeling of total peace, love for other beings—that all is right with the world.

There is always a tea break at some point in the class. This is a time for conversation or just resting. Especially for those who have known each other for a while, there may be some talk about where you are in your life. There may be camaraderie around a classmate's problems, but no ongoing therapy. There is often joking. There may be mention of the world's problems, but negative energy and too much analysis are avoided in order to maintain the stillness in the room. You learn more about Tai Chi philosophy in other chapters in this book; however, you may see just from this description how Tai Chi can be a stillness booster for you.

The Cedar Tree café

The Cedar Tree Café was a place for great coffee in Fredericton, the city where I work. Sadly, it is now closed, but for several years it was a special place for me. In the café atmosphere I imagine the spirit of existentialist writers I have studied including Jean-Paul Sartre and Ernest Hemingway. This means I felt relaxed there; I found stillness and peace in this setting. As with any good café, I also found it to be a place where I enjoyed writing. The owner, Lisa, created a lively and friendly atmosphere, yet you could find a quiet corner if you wanted.

This café was a refuge: it provided yet another way of getting out of my monkey mind, finding a break from the noise of my everyday thoughts and periodic emotional turbulence. The setting promoted stillness for me through the pleasure of relaxing alone with an excellent café latte, while engaging in some people watching, or reading my favourite newspaper, the British weekly *Telegraph*. There was stillness in company with a regular group who showed up for conversation. Over time, some of these café goers have become friends. Similar to the Tai Chi class, there was personal story sharing, but only to a point: a catching up, but no one monopolized the table. There was much humour, some of it outrageous. What I felt in this setting was that I was accepted and not judged, that we are all strong and frail at the same time, and that we can treasure each other's company on the journey. Some of us now continue this stillness practice at another location in town, Café Loka, and I seek out similar refuges when I travel.

Breakfast at the point

Breakfast is another refuge. Early in the morning, my wife, Liz, often makes a breakfast sandwich while I make café lattes, and we bike down to a little park on the ocean and sit on a bench. We sit quietly and enjoy the calm and the peace that comes from being in nature. One morning we saw four eagles; at other times there are ducks, loons, and small boats coming and going. We might calmly discuss something that is going on in her life or mine, but one of us always says at some point, "Okay, now let's just enjoy the moment."

Another interesting feature of a refuge is that once it becomes a refuge for you, even just thinking about that stillness environment will make you feel good. Usually I visit the Trappists only twice a year, but I can get a stillness boost just anticipating the next visit. Similarly, I feel more calm just thinking about going to my next Tai Chi class. Now, of course, you have to actually go to the refuge regularly or this effect will weaken. But all you need for any refuge to work is to show up and give it a try.

Explore your Pathway

Take some time to make a list of actual and potential refuges in your life. If you wish, consider how to access new refuges, or further cultivate your existing pathways to stillness.

CHAPTER 29
Time Well Wasted

ON one trip to my favourite Trappist monastery, the Abbott paid me a visit in the dining room, as he often does with those on retreat. I asked him a question about the role of the monastery in the post-modern world. I said that there is a common view, even within the Catholic community, that monks and nuns just waste their time and that they really do nothing but pray, and that this is unproductive. He simply said, "And what is wrong with wasting time?"

These words have a very rich meaning. Everyone at the monastery has a job—by operating a farm, they are a self-supporting community. As noted elsewhere, they pray formally seven times each day, from 3:30 a.m. to 7:30 p.m. In my view, their philosophy parallels Tai Chi practice. Whether the monks are working or at prayer, they invite stillness into their being. While praying they are practicing movement in stillness, and while working they practice stillness in movement. Prayer is time well wasted; sometimes doing nothing can be good for you: it allows space for stillness to arise, with its gift of rest and serenity.

If, as my friend Glen says, "You are inclined to be always busy and feel guilty or afraid to stop," and yet you are uncomfortable with this picture, perhaps you might want to try a relax- into-stillness movement or two (found at the end of the book). At first it may feel strange that suddenly there is nothing to do and nowhere to go, that simply *being* is enough. You may want to run back to the noise and the chaos.

Stillness is where you come from, but it is a forgotten country. You need to learn to revisit this new/old home, trust it, and find moments of true rest in it. Then, with more stillness practice, you may learn to find it and trust it in the middle of the noise, seeing it as part of the chaos—seeing that it can give some balance and sanity to your life. Often life forces us to slow down, and it turns out to be good for us. You might consider stillness practice as a way of taking care of yourself without being forced. As my friend's doctor recently said, "You take good care of your car and give it a rest. Why not do the same for yourself?" (This, as I suggest in Chapter 20, could even be seen as a form of self-defence.) With practice, you may find that you can let go and let stillness be part of whatever situation you are in, whether dealing with your inside story or some outside one, at home, work, or elsewhere.

But there is still another paradox at work here. Stillness practice allows you to both rest *and* regenerate. It releases energy trapped by tension. So, it actually gives you *more* available energy. And by spending more time in the present moment, you become less distracted and more focused. Thus you get more done in the end with less effort. Stillness works! As the saying goes, life is short, so slow down.

Explore your Pathway

Give yourself permission to waste a little time, by doing a relax-into-stillness movement at the end of the book, or even just sitting still for a few minutes. Observe how you feel. But be patient, since if you are not accustomed to wasting time it may take some practice to find joy in this experience.

CHAPTER 30
The Witness

AS you learn in other chapters, there have been a couple of occasions in my life when I have experienced intense anxiety, to the point that I needed to be open to help. During these times, stillness was hidden from my view. However, during one of these periods (some years ago now), I read one book by Eckhart Tolle in which he talks about emotions as energized thoughts arising from the thinking mind. He suggests that you try to simply allow this energy to be there; watch it, but refrain from creating a big story around the experience. This is different from denying the anxiety, and also different from trying to control or fix the situation—fight or flight. Rather, it is an example of the *third way*, letting go and accepting that it is there, but not trying to define it or understand it.

I once heard a yoga teacher compare this act of *watching thoughts* to observing fish in an aquarium or watching moving icons on a screen saver. I attempted to do this, and I must say it worked; it helped me to not label the energy as fear and to think that my life as I knew it was over. I was simply observing intense vibrating energy. I did not feel completely relieved or at peace as a result of this practice, but I did feel that there was a space or some degree of stillness in addition to the problems I was facing at the time. My story now included stillness as well as the drama that was causing me intense pain. I still had the pain, but not the *additional* pain of resisting what was happening. I was no longer completely identifying with that drama. I was at least dimly aware that it was a drama, and there was some consolation in that experience. Somehow, my story got larger, and I was able to see my pain as a story that I had created.

CHAPTER 31
Barista Training

IN Chapter 28 ("My Refuges"), I speak about the Cedar Tree Café. The owner of this café is my friend Lisa. On one of my regular visits for coffee, I told her in passing that I had wanted to learn to be a barista for a long time. "You're on," she said. "I will train you." So, during that winter, I spent one morning a week as an apprentice barista. I would arrive at 7 a.m. The first day she explained a few basic issues about the espresso machine. She gave me this talk only at the beginning. Then she said, "The best way to learn is to do it, so get behind the machine."

At first, I was very nervous. I knew that there was much more to the art of coffee than meets the eye. But then I realized that this sounded just like a Tai Chi class, where we just try the movements without the interfering monkey mind and its doubts and fears. So I jumped in, thinking that I would try my best and see what happened. Each day Lisa took me through the steps involved in making good espresso: choice of beans, grinding, tamping, pulling the shot, frothing the milk, how to make different drinks, such as cappuccinos, lattes, and, since we are in Canada, what she called *Canadianos* (as opposed to Americanos). She was a very good teacher and this training worked out well for me.

Then, after some weeks, she said, "Okay, now you will serve customers in the morning." Again I was nervous. I had been a waiter many years ago, but this was more complicated, and you have to get all the steps in the process right, and in a very short period of time. Well, with help from the staff when it got busy, this went very well, too. I not only learned about coffee but I made new friends among the staff. Another interesting aspect of this experience was that sometimes students whom I teach at university would come in for coffee. They would look at me and say, "Oh, Dr. Kenyon, have you lost your job?" Other people I know in the community would say, "Haven't I seen you somewhere before?"

Being a barista is an art and I continue to refine my coffee skills. I now have a good machine at home and make espresso for friends and guests who stay at our B&B. Several of my friends will call me about something and I know they are fishing for an invitation for coffee. One good friend in particular, Geoff, often visits The Netherlands, a country that generally has great coffee. When he tastes my latte, he says that he feels that he is on his bicycle riding along the canals in Holland, and it is like a quick vacation. I think he would agree that this experience becomes one of his refuges. I also make coffee every morning for my toughest customer: my wife, Liz. She likes really good coffee, so I want to try to please her this way.

This chapter in my life began with a love of good coffee, curiosity, and a willingness to try something new. It has brought a new source of meaning to my life, new friends, and a stillness practice in that it brings pleasure to my friends and to me as I continue to practice this art. Also, as a gerontologist I try to practice what I preach: It is never too late to have a happy childhood, as American novelist Tom Robbins has said, and to try something new. New itineraries on the journey can bring fun, peace, and more stillness to your life.

CHAPTER 32
Walk in Nature

TAKE a walk—in a park, a forest, at the seaside, whatever is available to you. However, when you are in nature, try to refrain from labelling things. I have been for walks where my companions are into information. They'll tell you what kinds of trees, flowers, brush, and birds you are observing, or they are constantly taking photos. Unless I am on a guided tour, I find this quite disturbing. To find stillness in nature, try to observe your surroundings as if the objects and creatures had no names—they are just forms.

In this way, the thinking mind is put in the background and you are able to *feel* the stillness in nature. This is how nature speaks to you. It may take some practice, but showing up for nature is worth the effort. It reminds me of the scene in the film *Patch Adams* where Patch's fellow resident in the hospital holds up four fingers and asks Patch how many fingers he is holding up. After a few tries, Patch finally looks *through* the fingers, not at them, and gets the correct answer: eight. He is no longer seeing with his thinking mind.

The tree

A setting in which I have the privilege to create conditions for the emergence of stillness is a credit course which I teach to undergraduate students at St. Thomas University. The course is entitled *Aging and Tai Chi*. The usual assignments are part of the course—article reviews, tests, and a reflection paper. However, the students also practise Tai Chi. They learn a set of movements and breathing techniques called Chi Kung. These are similar to the relax-into- stillness movements in this book, and we perform them in both standing and seated positions. The instructions emphasize letting go, relaxing, not competing, and dropping the monkey mind. Most of the students have never experienced this type of course, and it is an adjustment from the usual exclusive emphasis on information and intellectual reasoning—in other words, on the thinking mind.

Here is a story told to me by one of the students in the class, recounted with her

permission. It demonstrates both the availability of stillness and its wonderful possibilities:

> Growing up, I had never been interested in any form of organized athleticism. From an early age I preferred climbing trees, swimming, running, and exploring the outdoors in complete solitude. Due to having an abusive father as a child, I was always trying to escape the hostility and noise that I associated with home. It seemed as though my mind was already on overload, and high-intensity games such as soccer would only push me into having a mental

breakdown! So instead of seeking out competitive, tense, and high-speed sports, I drifted toward what I consider "premature meditation."

I would spend every minute that my father was home exploring the thirteen acres of country land that my family owned. I had invested a lot of time in constructing a tree fort in our back woods. I spent even more time running in our field aimlessly and throwing rocks down by our brook. I remember entire days that I would dedicate to just climbing trees and taking refuge in their branches. My memories of tree climbing as a child are my absolute favourite.

In those hours, I was most calm and most focused. It is almost amusing to me that those memories are recollected more vividly than memories of my birthday parties and family get-togethers. I believe that is because in those moments, I was not attempting to ignore reality. In those moments I was safe and did not have to block out any pain.

To me, that is the key dynamic of meditation—being entirely aware of internal and external conditions without constant analyzations hindering the sense of calm. I know that is why I have enjoyed this Introduction to Tai Chi class so passionately. In spite of my ups and downs, I have re-experienced those calm and simple moments from childhood once more. I have found my tree!

Explore your Pathway

The next time you can, go to a park, the woods, the seaside, somewhere quiet in nature. Turn off your devices. Try a relax-into-stillness movement. Then sit quietly and listen and feel what is around you. Let nature share its stillness with you, rather than you trying to do something with it.

CHAPTER 33
Elaine's Left Knee

ACCEPTANCE of your situation brings you to the present moment where stillness resides. And it is out of this acceptance that you are able to *restory*, to find new meaning and moments of peace. This is because, in the moment of acceptance, you have ceased resistance; you have suspended the effort to control and fix the situation with your monkey mind. You have stopped attempting to engineer a solution to your problem. The following story is from Elaine, a former student in my Death and Dying class:

> While on the subject of high school, I'd like to touch on an experience that had a major impact on my life. In Chapter 2 of the textbook, we discuss phenomenological death. This kind of death comes from the inside—a reflection of yourself, a "disconnection" from your story. During the discussion of this section, I immediately was reminded of my knee injury in grade eleven. It was May 17, the day before my eighteenth birthday. I was playing

rugby on my home field, and it was only my third game ever. I was feeling bold and wanted to try a new sport, and I was never scared of a little aggression (even though I was the smallest player on the team). I had scored what they call a "try" (a goal) through an interception in my very first game, and this boosted my confidence—looking back, a little more than it should have. I was running with the ball, and had one more player to beat. When she grabbed me, I fought the tackle as hard as I could by planting my foot firmly into the ground. When my body twisted, my knee was done for. It was a shocking moment, because I had never experienced pain like that in my whole life.

It turned out to be a torn ACL, which required a surgery and a six-month recovery period. This eliminated my entire graduating year of sports. I had been playing soccer and basketball since the age of four, and being an athlete was all I had ever known. I was miserable, to say the least, as I watched all of my best friends on the field and on the court. I became a very bitter and emotional person. However, it came down to a point where I decided I had to do something to make up for it, because I could no longer sit on the sidelines and feel sorry for myself. I went through my own five stages of loss, looking back. Now that I know what they are, they were surprisingly accurate (denial, anger, bargaining, depression, acceptance). Once I reached acceptance, what did I do? I decided to run for valedictorian of my graduating class, and I won. On graduation day, I delivered the best speech I'd ever delivered to date, in front of an easy couple of thousand people. I was so proud of myself, and that's where my true recovery began.

That summer, I worked as hard as I could to get back on the field. I went to physiotherapy three times a week and did all my exercises religiously. After the long six-month wait, I was back on the field (with a knee brace, of course). Things only went up from there. I made a last-minute decision to come to this university. I was a walk-on at soccer tryouts, and I made the team as a first-year. Continuing my athletics and not giving up after my injury was the best decision I've ever made. I just finished my second season with the school team—and I no longer need my knee brace! This just goes to show how one must accept their new reality and keep moving forward from whatever loss they have experienced—in my case, the loss of use of my left knee.

Elaine's story reminds us that change occurs at all points in the journey to life and that we can learn from each other regardless of the number of years we have been on this planet.

Explore your Pathway

Elaine's story is inspiring; however, it is not easy or always possible to accept unwanted changes in life. Still, you might try to be open to other stories about what is happening to you. And, you can try to step back and relax into stillness.

CHAPTER 34
Stacking Wood

THERE are times when I can observe that I am living out of stillness. For example, one day I had to stack two cords of split firewood at a friend's home. We had purchased the wood together and he was storing some of it for me. It had to be done on that day because it was going to rain for the following several days. The problem was that I had twisted my knee a few days earlier and I could hardly walk. Now, I tend to get anxious about situations like this and think up all kinds of potential problems. Will I be able to move the wheelbarrow fifty times up and down the hill of the driveway? Will I get it all done before the rain starts? If it is not done, my friend cannot park his car in the driveway.

However, on that day I was able to stay in the present moment. I put a brace on my knee, and just went over to do the job. I began slowly and tried to be careful moving the wheelbarrow full of wood. It was not too bad, but after a while I could feel the knee weakening. I decided I would just do as much as I could and not worry about it. It was shortly after this reflection that my friend's daughter, son-in-law, and granddaughter showed up for a visit. They jumped in to help. The wood was done within the next hour and my knee was no longer an issue. In fact, later that day I helped the same friend move a piano.

This everyday example shows that if you are able to just stay in the moment and not jump to the future, you never know how the universe will unfold. My anxiety over this situation would have been wasted energy and unnecessary suffering—but not from the knee. Being able to stay in the moment like this is not something I can always control. I believe it comes from regular practice of relaxing into stillness. Eventually, the practice spills over into daily life. And then, when you experience stillness in your daily life, you remember how it feels, and can more easily call it up next time.

Bike and kayak meditation

What follows is a story from a student, Christine, about another way to find stillness. Prior to my class on Aging and Tai Chi, she had experience with various types of physical activity, including biking and kayaking.

> To demonstrate the ways in which these activities may be seen as a form of meditation, I will discuss the activity in which I have' participated the most: biking. When I am biking I do not focus on the past or the future (such as the destination), but rather I'm able to focus on the moment, my surroundings, and my body. For example, when I was in high school, I would, on occasion, bike [80 km] from my hometown of Rexton to Moncton and,

on some occasions, bike back the same day. During these bike rides my focus was not on the destination but on the moment, the scenery around me, and the energy within my legs. As such, time seemed to elude me, and before I even realized the time had passed, I was in Moncton. In this way, I am able to "calm" or "drop below" my "monkey mind" or "thinking mind" and reduce my anxieties that have resulted from worrying about the past and the future.

Kayaking is another prominent form of meditation in my life. Similar to biking, when I am kayaking I feel as if I am present within the moment. I experience my body, its strengths and weaknesses, the movements of the water, the freshness of the air, the reflection of the mirror-like water (on calm days), and the coolness of the water beneath me in contrast to the warmth of the sun. In these activities, I am able to return myself to the present moment and experience life as it is at the moment, rather than how it has been or how it might be.

Spiritual biking

Jack is a friend of mine who is a Catholic priest, currently in his mid-eighties. He is also a colleague at St. Thomas University where I teach. Jack has been a guest lecturer in my Aging and Spirituality class for many years. On one of these visits he was telling us about how we need to be open to the workings of our personal spiritual journey. He told us that a few years earlier he was going through a serious depressive period, feeling a lack of meaning and purpose after decades of being a priest and a university professor. He was feeling the *no-way-out* experience that suffering often brings (which you learn about in the chapter, "Meaningful Suffering?").

One evening, while he was watching television with nothing better to do, a show about cycling caught his attention. It came to him that he had always been interested in this activity, but had never attempted it. He did not understand why he was motivated to do so now, but he decided to give it a try nonetheless. So he rented a bicycle and began riding a few blocks at a time. Gradually, he increased the distance. He then hooked up with some other cyclists in town. Eventually, he found himself touring in Europe, meeting new friends, and feeling happy again.

By following this gut feeling, Jack regained his sense of meaning and purpose. He was able to return to being an enthusiastic priest and to restory his way to stillness. The lesson you can learn from Jack's story is that everything about you can be part of your pathway to stillness. By being open to the possibilities around you and not resisting or putting restrictions on which options are correct or appropriate to your inner life—"I am too old to cycle!" "This is not prayer or a religious activity!"—you too can find stillness on your meandering journey to life.

When it comes to biking in particular, my good friend Geoff, who is an artist, considers it to be the magic pill. He is mainly an off-road cyclist, and finds that when he is biking things get very quiet, stillness happens, and he is able to allow creative insights to emerge—not just for his paintings, but also for personal and professional decisions. But this is not all. Geoff tells me that after a couple of hours on the trails, all his stress disappears. For him, biking is a stillness practice.

Explore your Pathway

Try a "relax into stillness" movement at the end of the book. Then, allow your imagination to wander (not your thinking mind with its doubts and objections) and write down activities that are or could be stillness practices in your life. As a second step, you might consider how the stillness you find in these practices is important to your daily life. This second step adds to the motivation factor when you remind yourself about how much better life is when you do your practice.

CHAPTER 35
Floating Shoes

HERE is a stillness story contributed by my wife Liz:

At the time of my stillness experience, I was working in a cubicle for the government. It was a job where I felt enclosed, stifled, and not free—rather trapped by the paycheque and the "security." There was no creativity allowed, only policies implemented. It was so against my soul and who I was to be working in a government cubicle, but I had made a career choice that I did not realize was against everything I was as a person. I was in denial and plodded along day after day, just like I was in a trance or living someone else's life. I needed to be free and creative, and this was not the place.

A friend who saw and felt my unhappiness and discontent told me about a painting course that was to be held in St. Andrews by the Sea. It was a week-long workshop where participants would be painting outside—*plein air* is the artist term. At first I thought, *I could never do this—who am*

I? Just a government employee, surely not an artist. What would the other artists think of me and my lost ability to be creative? As a younger person, I loved to paint and write poetry, but that had long been buried in the responsibilities of life, children, household duties, and jobs for money.

I decided and also needed to take a chance—a beginning step, a new path—so I enrolled for the *Plein Air* course. On the second day of the course we were to paint the sea and sailboats. I located myself on a beach while the tide was far out and was painting the boats in the distance. I sat in my new painting chair (with a sun umbrella attached to it) and was wearing a new sunhat. Paints in hand, I looked at the blank paper and took a deep breath. The seagulls were gliding in the clear, blue sky above me. The sultry, salt air, warmed by the sun, was wonderfully fresh. I could not believe where I was—out in nature, in the open expanse of the sea and the beach. I took my shoes off and felt the sand on my bare feet, and experienced a real connection to Mother Earth and all her healing properties. I began to paint the sky and sailboats. All time stood still; I felt free and ageless, excited about what lay ahead, and so very grateful.

All of a sudden I heard someone yelling and calling my name. It was my art teacher, running from afar towards me and shouting, "Liz, Liz! Your shoes—your shoes! They are floating away!" I had not realized that the tide had come in—all the way up to my chair—as I had no semblance of time. Time had literally stopped for me while I was painting. What a wonderful discovery! At least three hours had gone by and I had been in a place called "stillness." Just me and my "seeing brain" observing nature and becoming creative again.

From that day on, I knew it did not matter if I was an "artiste" or not; what *did* matter was that painting allowed me to rest in this stillness, in this connection with creativity that I had lost for so many years. I was able to see and feel again how the open space of nature is my stillness nurturer.

Liz's story reminds us that we can be guided on our pathway through the realization that our present journey is no longer meaningful and is even causing us pain. This realization can prompt us to seek something new without knowing exactly where we are going, but knowing that we can no longer stay where are. Yet, we still need to make the decision to get on the train to the new destination, to show up for the train. Being an artist is now part of Liz's pathway to stillness. As a result of the floating shoes, and painting now being an important stillness practice for her, Liz exhibits her work across Canada.

CHAPTER 36
St. Therese of Lisieux

ST. Therese is a Catholic saint who lived in France in the nine-teenth century. She entered a convent at age fifteen and died at twenty-four. During much of her time in the convent, she was seri-ously ill, lived in a cold and damp environment, and was treated badly by her fellow nuns. She is known for her devotion to the little child Jesus and her spiritual path of becoming child-like. Childlike does not mean *childish*. For Therese, it was a matter of complete acceptance of what was coming her way, and trusting everything to Jesus. In letting go, she opened a space that invited stillness into her suffering. This brought a measure of comfort and solace to her life, rather than being completely overwhelmed by pain. In this way, she was able to restory her pain so that she was not totally stuck in it. Somehow she trusted that there was a purpose for her pain, even though her thinking mind could not understand it.

Similarly, Brother Leo, my friend at the Trappist monastery, says that he would rather God give him his suffering now and get it over with, because he believes that learning to accept his suffering will bring him eventual peace. St. Therese found stillness by surrendering her suffering to God. She did not seek suffering as many religious seekers did in earlier times. It might be that there is no gain from seeking pain, as looking for trouble may just strengthen the ego with a sense of "Look at me—I can take that."

St. Therese was able to develop a stillness practice through her metaphor of the little child: open, vulnerable, loving, yet able to accept intense pain. She did not pray for this or that to happen; she just accepted. In fact, her *little-child* path to stillness was severely tested at the end of her life. In addition to serious illness—and after a life of total dedication to God and her fellow human beings—she experienced a period of atheism, of intense doubt of her faith. I believe this was a spiritual experience, because she had to drop all her thinking-mind beliefs about the nature of stillness in order to be truly free in the experience of stillness. It is also the meaning of the Buddhist saying, "If you meet the Buddha on the road, kill him."

When you are in doubt, it is not stillness that is in question, but your story about how you understand stillness. You need the words as signposts, but you also need to move on from the sign to the real thing. Becoming small can create room for stillness to be an active part of who you are. On a lighter note, you may recall Sergeant Schultz on the television show *Hogan's Heroes*. He used to say, "I know nothing; I hear nothing; I see nothing." By adopting this philosophy, he kept himself out of trouble. Rather than being an indication of weakness and immaturity, becoming childlike may be a sign of real strength and maturity—and, most importantly, a pathway to wisdom and stillness in your life.

Explore your Pathway

At first glance, the story of St. Therese seems, especially to the stereotypical male, like the antithesis of what we need to get through this life; strength, control, power. However, you might want to consider how the "little child" metaphor can be seen as "the real macho". It takes great courage to accept, trust and let go. You may discover that stillness is found in the space that is left after we leave behind the baggage of our ego and its illusion of control.

CHAPTER 37
A Sunlit Absence

A *Sunlit Absence* is the inspiring title of a book by Martin Laird. It is a lovely way to express stillness. This phrase helps me embrace the idea that taking *things* away—whether the outside world or my own thoughts and emotions—does not mean that there is nothing left. It is difficult to contemplate that there can be a fullness in emptiness, that there is light rather than darkness, lightness rather than heaviness. I read somewhere that stillness hides in silence. For me, stillness as a sunlit absence is most intensely experienced in my refuge of solitary practice, which includes sitting meditation and Tai Chi practice. Interestingly, I can also feel this way when I am teaching Tai Chi to my dementia survivor friends. It is a shared stillness that we co-create with soft music, relax-into-stillness movements, and the voice of silence.

When I am *in the zone*, I feel a strong sense of peace and warmth. I feel safe and comforted. I feel that there is nothing that needs to be done and nowhere I need to go. The burden lightens both physically and emotionally. Thoughts, feelings, and life stresses come and go. I am reminded to be gentle with my practice, to simply follow and return to my breath. Like water that flows around rocks—even through them, over time—slipping into crevices, appearing and disappearing, finally to its destination, I feel that our journey inevitably winds its way to stillness.

CHAPTER 38
Lost and Found

THIS stillness story, written by my good friend Ardeth, occupies the proverbial last but by far not least place in this book.

Stillness . . .
I swing and sway, whirl and twirl,
As I dance with the sunbeams
In a field of daisies.

My eyes open to a tunnel of love,
Where leaves on the tree's whisper,
Come in, little child, come in . . .

Each step takes me deeper . . .
Until there is only
Me.

I listen.
A gurgling brook,
A breeze whistling in the treetops,
Birds twitter,
A branch snaps,
The smell of dampness.

All there in the midst
Of the forest primordial.

A ray of light beams down on me.

I understand.

Be still.

And know
that
I
am
God.

Stillness Lost . . .
Be here, go there, learn this, do that.
Work, work, work—eight hours, now twelve.
Work—more hours, more hours, more hours.
No time.
Overwhelmed.

Volunteer. Family needs. A to-do list that
Stretches from here to eternity.

One day, something happens.
One day, an illness.
Another day, a death.
Another pulled by guilt, fear, ego.

One day, the knowing.
I can't do *this* anymore.
What IS *THIS*?

Ahhhhhh . . .
THIS IS the absence of
Stillness.

Where did it go?
When did I lose it?
How did this happen?
Why did this happen?

The journey began . . .
Who am I?

The twists and turns? Wonderful teachers!
Time invested? Priceless.

Lost in the wilderness.
Found within—the core of
Who
I
Am.

Stillness Found . . .

Be Still . . . and know
that
I
Am
God.

God is a state of . . .
BE---ING.

BE---ING the Spirit of Divine within.

In the BE-GINNING was
Nature.

Millions of years later . . .
Human BE---INGS.

I weep for nature lost . . .
The forest primordial,
Our external reminder of . . .
Divine
Within.

Stillness.

Peace.

Perfect Peace.

I am.

How Divine!

EPILOGUE

I find that as my journey continues, I am more aware of my *stillness barometer*. This means that I am increasingly sensitive to the level of stillness in my experiences with what Buddhists call *the ten thousand things*. The ten thousand things refer to people, places, and situations I encounter, and include my own thoughts and emotions. As my stillness level increases through my stillness practice, I find that I am less likely to want to choose situations that pull me away from that stillness, and, conversely, I seek out those that increase my stillness level. I like and prefer the feeling of stillness. Buddhists also say that at some point these ten thousand things become one, and then we return to the origin where we have always been. We are able to reside in stillness *within* the ten thousand things.

I believe this is true, but for me it remains a destination that continues to be elusive. As we learned throughout this book, it is not even a destination that you can *seek*. You can only show up for the train and enjoy the existential ride. There is a memorial plaque to Courtney Estes, a late acquaintance, on a bench in the sculpture garden at Kingsbrae Garden in St. Andrews. The words on the plaque are, "Life is not about waiting for the storm to pass, it is about learning to dance in the rain." I believe that we all need to—and are able to get better at—dancing in the rain. As I finish writing this book, I ask: What can we do in the face of the ten thousand things that include mass migration, mindless acts of terror, a problematic world economy, and climate change, along with our own personal and social challenges?

First, we can remind ourselves that the ten thousand things also include love, compassion, wisdom, and the beauty of nature. And second, this book urges that you try to let go, relax into stillness, and find your own pathway to stillness. At times you may need to seek out these practices more frequently, perhaps even hourly. There is so much that we cannot control, but we can still dance in the rain, and raise the level of our stillness barometers.

RELAX
into Stillness Movements

Movement 1: Wu Chi

Wu Chi is a standing meditation position.

1. Stand with your feet shoulder width apart.
2. Release your hips and your knees. (In the seated version, place your hands on your thighs and follow the remainder of the instructions.) The idea in Tai Chi is to never have your joints in a locked position.
3. Place your tongue lightly at the roof of your mouth. Arms and shoulders hang naturally, not folded and not held back military style.
4. Gently curl your fingers. Your chest should feel relaxed.
5. Tuck your chin slightly to try to suspend the crown of your head.

6. Breathe in and out through the nose.

7. Now observe your breath gently coming in and out of your stomach area, and enjoy the stillness.

Movement 2: The Wave

1. Give yourself a rest; find a quiet place for even five minutes. At work, I close my office door, turn off the phone and computer. It may sound strange, but I have been known to close the door to the bathroom in a hotel room to find these five minutes of stillness.

2. Stand with your feet shoulder width (or remain seated). Gently coordinate your in-breath with your arms floating up, palms up, and the out-breath with arms floating down, palms down.

3. Turn the palms over at shoulder height and float down as you breathe out, as if you are trailing through water. Without forcing, try to breathe from the stomach area, and relax your stomach on the out-breath. Relax your shoulders and keep your elbows loose.

4. Awareness of the movement itself, along with the breath, is very effective in calming the monkey mind and bringing you to stillness.

5. Repeat at least five times as slowly as you feel comfortable. You may picture a wave coming in and out as you raise and lower your arms.

Movement 3: Cloud Hands

1. Begin with the Wave movement shown on the previous page.
2. Cross your wrists at the bottom of the wave; turn palms up; raise your arms in a circle until palms are facing you at chest level.
3. Turn palms over and complete the circle.
4. Repeat three times with normal breathing.
5. On the fourth circle, use a full breath.
6. Without forcing, breathe from the stomach area and relax your stomach on the out-breath.
7. Close your eyes and imagine your arms floating up and moving on their own through the circles.
8. Repeat the complete movement five times or as you are comfortable.

SUGGESTED READINGS

Bianchi, E. (1995). *Aging as a Spiritual Journey*. New York: Crossroad.

Black, H. (2006). *Soul Pain: The Meaning of Suffering in Later Life*. Amityville, NY: Baywood.

Brody, H. (1994). "My story is broken; can you help me fix it?" Medical ethics and the joint construction of narrative. *Literature and Medicine*. 13 (1), 79–92.

Chödrön, P. (1994). *Start Where You Are: A Guide to Compassionate Living*. Boston, MA: Shambala.

Dalai Lama (2001). *An Open Heart: Practicing Compassion in Everyday Life*. Boston, MA: Little, Brown.

Dalai Lama, & Chan, V. (2004). *The Wisdom of Forgiveness*. New York: Riverhead Books.

Das, S. (1997). *Awakening the Buddha Within*. New York: Broadway Books.

Drew, L., & Ferrari, L. (2005). *Different Minds: Living with Alzheimer Disease*. Fredericton, NB: Goose Lane Editions.

Frankl, V. (1962). *Man's Search for Meaning*. New York: Simon and Schuster.

Huxley, A. (1962). *The Perennial Philosophy*. Cleveland, OH: Meridian.

Iyer, P. (2014). *The Art of Stillness*. New York: Simon and Schuster.

Kabat-Zinn, J. (2009). *Full Catastrophe Living*. New York: Bantam Dell.

Kenyon, G., Bohlmeijer, E., & Randall, W. (Eds.). (2011). *Storying Later Life: Issues, Investigations, and Interventions in Narrative Gerontology*. New York: Oxford University Press.

Klein, B. (1984). *Movements of Magic: The Spirit of T'ai-Chi-Ch'uan*. North Hollywood, CA: Newcastle.

Kübler-Ross, E. (1969). *On Death and Dying*. New York: Scribner.

Kuhl, D. (2002). *What Dying Patients Want: Practical Wisdom at the End of Life*. New York: Perseus.

Laird, M. (2011). *A Sunlit Absence: Silence, Awareness, and Contemplation*. New York: Oxford University Press.

Marcel, G. (1962). *Homo Viator*. New York: Harper and Row.

Merton, T. (1996). *Contemplative Prayer*. New York: Doubleday.

Ming, L. (2006). *Awakening to the Tao*. Boston: Shambala.

Mitchell, S. (1988). *Tao Te Ching*. New York: HarperCollins.

Moore, T. (1994). *Meditations on the Monk Who Dwells in Daily Life*. New York: HarperCollins.

Randall, W., & Kenyon, G. (2001). *Ordinary Wisdom: Biographical Aging and the Journey of Life*. Westport, CT: Praeger.

Nhat Hanh, T. (1999). *Going Home: Jesus and Buddha as Brothers*. New York: Riverhead.

Nhat Hanh, T. (2007). *Nothing to Do, Nowhere to Go: Waking Up to Who You Are*. Berkeley, CA: Parallax.

Nouwen, H. (1986). *Reaching Out: The Three Movements of the Spiritual Life*. New York: Doubleday.

O'Donohue, J. (2005). *Beauty: The Invisible Embrace*. New York: HarperCollins Perennial.

Petitot, H. (1927). *Saint Teresa of Lisieux: A Spiritual Renascence*. London: Burns Oates & Washbourne.

Rinpoche, S. (1994). *The Tibetan Book of Living and Dying*. San Francisco, CA: HarperSanFrancisco.

St. Therese of Lisieux (1997). *The Story of a Soul*. Rockford, IL: Tan Books and Publishers.

Tolle, E. (2003). *Stillness Speaks*. Vancouver: Namaste.

Tolle, E. (2005). *A New Earth: Awakening to Your Life's Purpose*. Toronto: Penguin.

Vanier, J. (2005). *Befriending the Stranger*. Toronto: Novalis.

Wild, R. (1978). *Word from Poustinia.* Denville, NJ:
Dimension Books.

Zee, W. (2002). *Wu Style Tai Chi Chuan.* Berkeley, CA: North
Atlantic Books.

Follow Me:
BLOG-PathwaysToStillness.org
FB-TWTR-@garyirwinkenyon
Instagram-garyirwinkenyon

ABOUT THE AUTHOR

GARY Irwin-Kenyon is founding Chair and Professor, Gerontology Department, St. Thomas University, Fredericton, New Brunswick, Canada. He is a Fellow of the Andrew Norman Institute for Advanced Studies in Gerontology and Geriatrics, University of Southern California. Dr. Irwin-Kenyon is listed in Who's Who in Canada (Grey House Publishing) and the United States (Marquis Biographies Online). He has authored, co-authored or co-edited six books, including *Narrative Gerontology, Storying Later Life, Restorying Your Life,* and *Ordinary Wisdom.* Dr. Irwin-Kenyon is a teacher and practitioner of Tai Chi with more than thirty years experience. He designed a programme, *Tai Chi as Narrative Care,* which he has been teaching for the past ten years to special groups, including residents in long-term care. He conducts workshops and seminars in Canada, The United States, Europe, and Asia. Dr. Irwin-Kenyon is also an apprentice barista. He resides in St. Andrews by the Sea, New Brunswick, Canada with his wife Liz, where they operate Seahaven, an organic B&B.